PENGUIN BOOKS

MORE SPIKE MILLIGAN LETTERS

Spike Milligan was born at Ahmednagar in India in 1919. He received his first education in a tent in the Hyderabad Sindh desert and graduated from there, through a series of Roman Catholic schools in India and England, to the Lewisham Polytechnic. Always something of a playboy, he then plunged into the world of Show Business, seduced by his first stage appearance, at the age of eight, in the nativity play of his Poona convent school. He began his career as a band musician but has since become famous as a humorous script writer and actor in both films and broadcasting. He was one of the main figures in and behind the infamous Goon Show. Among the films he has appeared in are: *Suspect*, *Invasion*, *Postman's Knock* and *Milligan at Large*.

Spike Milligan has also published *The Little Potboiler*, *Silly Verse for Kids*, *Dustbin of Milligan*, *A Book of Bits*, *The Bed-Sitting Room* (a play), *The Bald Twit Lion*, *A Book of Milliganimals*, *Small Dreams of a Scorpion*, *Transports of Delight* and his war memoirs, *Adolf Hitler: My Part in His Downfall*, *'Rommel?' 'Gunner Who?'*, *Monty: His Part in My Victory* and *Mussolini: His Part in My Downfall*. Among his other publications are *The Milligan Book of Records, Games, Cartoons and Commercials*, *Dip the Puppy*, *William McGonagall: The Truth at Last* (with Jack Hobbs), *The Spike Milligan Letters*, edited by Norma Farnes, *Open Heart University*, *The Q Annual*, *Unspun Socks from a Chicken's Laundry* and *The 101 Best and Only Limericks of Spike Milligan*.

Norma Farnes: Editor, manager, agent, banker, accountant, secretary, typist, receptionist, relief switchboard girl, housekeeper, cook, shopper, duty-runner, schlepper, confidante, angel, saint, and tough cookie.

More
Spike Milligan
Letters

Edited by Norma Farnes

PENGUIN BOOKS

Penguin Books Ltd, Harmondsworth, Middlesex, England
Viking Penguin Inc., 40 West 23rd Street, New York 10010, U.S.A.
Penguin Books Australia Ltd, Ringwood, Victoria, Australia
Penguin Books Canada Ltd, 2801 John Street, Markham, Ontario, Canada L3R 1B4
Penguin Books (N.Z.) Ltd, 182–190 Wairau Road, Auckland 10, New Zealand

First published by M. & J. Hobbs and Michael Joseph 1984
Published in Penguin Books 1985

Made and printed in Great Britain by
Butler & Tanner Ltd, Frome and London

I dedicate this book, with love, to
JACK CLARKE

Contents

'Spike Who?' (1961)

Introduction

Extract from foreword of last book by Spike: '. . . and I will be back in the office next Monday morning working for her as usual.' And so six years on nothing has changed, except that perhaps I have aged sixteen years and Spike looks not a day older.

I explained in the introduction of the first book of letters just how I came to edit that book. Another book – another explanation.

I had promised Spike the first copy. When it arrived, after looking through it I gave it to him, explaining, 'It's not exactly as I had planned – look at page 79, and 115, I think that's really tatty.' This was in reference to a drawing of a hand, with a finger pointing over the page. I wanted captions underneath the pictures on the same page. Being Spike he was perspicacious enough to realise that I was genuinely upset about it. He said, 'Listen to me. When you hand in a book to the publishers, the first person that gets his hands on it cocks it up 10%, *then* the designer gets his hands on it and *he* cocks it up 10%, and if it stops there, you're bloody lucky.'

I said: 'Spike, it's OK for you, but this is possibly the only book I'll ever do, and I wanted it to be so right. You do so many books, you get more cracks at the whip.' Spike replied typically, 'Don't let them beat you – do another one.' And this is it.

I was pleasantly surprised at the reaction I received from the first book. As I said at the time, 'I've tried to capture the many facets of Spike', and judging by the mail I received from his many fans, I think I succeeded to a certain degree.

Six years on I'm still being asked the same question – is he mad? I have never thought so. As he gets older – though physically he is like a much younger man – I realise he will naturally be cast as one of those growing rarities, an English eccentric. He has the necessary Irish antecedents to qualify. The essential ingredient of the truly dotty eccentric is that he believes everything he does is logical, utterly sane and above all ordinary.

For example, Spike loves butterflies. His garden, near some woods, has none. He knows butterflies like nettles. The garden of my house in Yorkshire is surrounded by nettles and abounds in butterflies. The fact that his own woods are thick with nettles is beside the point. He asked me to bring some nettles down from Yorkshire for him and I didn't think it was that extraordinary until I asked one of the locals, a man that knows absolutely everything about the countryside, Alan Duck, if he would get me some really good nettles, with strong roots, to take back to London. It was only his reply, which is completely unprintable, which made me realise just how funny it was. Alan got me the nettles, I brought them back to London on the train and then they went off in a taxi to Spike's home in Hadley Common and were planted immediately. To Spike these were precious butterfly-attracting nettles and worth every penny of the taxi fare. Mind you, the locals are still talking about it six months later.

Spike travels all over the world and loathes baggage collection at airports, so he takes only hand luggage. 'Why does anybody travel any other way?' he asks. He buys what he needs when he arrives and gives it away before he leaves.

A few years ago we were going to Canada on a business trip for four days. When we met at the airport he asked, 'What's that?', pointing to my suitcase. 'You'll never see it again and when we get to Toronto you'll be standing at the conveyor belt, your head going around in unison with the belt, and when the last suitcase comes up on the belt and it's not yours, then the fun will start.' I said exasperatedly, 'Oh Spike.'

At Toronto we were being met by Lawrence Drizen and his wife Esther. When they knew we were going over there Esther had rung me and asked if I would bring her a side of Scotch smoked salmon, which I did, strapped to my suitcase. Well . . . there was I, my head going in unison with the conveyor belt, Spike had given up waiting and was sitting down as far away as possible. Five minutes later, a voice came over my shoulder (he does a very good impersonation of me), in the same exasperated tone saying, 'Oh Spike . . .' He was right. The luggage plus the salmon had gone 'somewhere' but certainly not to Toronto. Spike walked out of the airport, clutching his blue canvas hand luggage with a smile on his face. Esther Drizen had to loan me some night clothes and I spent two hours on the phone in the hotel trying to trace my luggage. The next day it turned up at the hotel, with Spike still going around saying, 'Oh Spike! Oh Spike!'

A few years ago, Spike had a telephone call from John Varty who runs the Londolozi Game Reserve in South Africa, to say that they were culling elephants in the Kruger Park. They needed Spike's help to translocate the elephants to the Londolozi. It cost £1500 to translocate one elephant. Day-to-day business stopped. Spike wrote letters. Whoever paid the £1500 would have the right to have an elephant tagged and choose a name for it: 'You can name an elephant yourself and have a certificate, stating the fact, and you yourself will always know there is an elephant with your name tag on it running free somewhere in Africa.' The money poured in, from Paul and Linda McCartney, the Bee Gees, who bought an elephant each, Elton John, Peter Sellers – then, thank God, normal business could be resumed. Recently, four years after the event, Spike was at the Londolozi Game Reserve and heard that Elton John was at the Mala Mala Game Reserve nearby. He didn't telephone Elton John at the Mala Mala, he telephoned me in London: 'Why hasn't Elton come to the Londolozi to see his elephant? He must have forgotten. Ring him, remind him.' Elton was reminded, via London.

I've enjoyed collating these letters, and I do hope that Spike's fans get as much pleasure from them as they obviously did from the first collection.

Norma Farnes

Acknowledgements

I would like to thank all the contributors in this book who gave their permission to publish their letters and photographs.

A special thanks to Tanis Davies for all her help, not just with this book, but for tolerating me over the last fifteen years, and to Groucho Matthews, Spike's No. 1 Fan, for his kindness to me.

The author and publishers would like to thank the following for permission to reproduce their photographs and illustrations: Mark Gerson (pages 6 and 113), Central Independent Television (p. 33), Tate & Lyle (p. 50), Larry Ellis (p. 60), Camera Press (p. 86), Pete Clarke (pp. 98–99), the Decca Recording Company (p. 103), the BBC (p. 116), David Edwards, BBC (p. 158), New Zealand *Herald & Weekly News* (p. 161), Benn Gunn (p. 195) and Chris Lord (p. 202). Every effort has been made to attribute illustrations accurately, and we apologise for any omissions.

At the Bayswater Loony Bin Again

POST ✦ OFFICE

TELEGRAM

Prefix. Time handed in. Office of origin and Service Instructions. Words.

No._____

OFFICE STAMP

RECEIVED

From ___ *Mo'*

By _____

To030 FLB9836 0AF616 TF1019 GBXX CO AASV _____ m

019 SYDNEY 19/18 30 1211

To _____

By _____

N FARNES   BAYSWATERLONDONW2UK

ARRIVING LONDON SIX FORTY AM FLIGHT QF1 PLEASE
ARRANGE TRANSPORT   S MILLIGAN

COL N 9 QF1   TS15/104 LN ✠

For free repetition of doubtful words telephone "TELEGRAMS ENQUIRY" or call, with this form
at office of delivery. Other enquiries should be accompanied by this form, and, if possible, the envelope.

B or C

Typical telegram. The game: guess the date.

URGENT

15/1/82
4-25 p.m.

DON MOUSSEAU. ORIGINAL
RECORDS. REMEMBER HIM?
PLEASE TALK TO ME
ABOUT "STICKY ON MY
FINGERS." I was here—
where were you?
Mark Thatcher is safe.
His Car Insurance has
gone up

Buttons arrived in the mail to Spike without a letter.

'GOD KNOWS WHAT
THESE BUTTONS ARE FOR.
hola

With the Compliments of

Maxwell Vine

For Putting on clothes dear!

7, Sackville Street,
London. W.1

15

I had said, 'Go on a cruise, it will do you good. You need the rest.' – Hence
'*Now* what?'

S. JORGE (Madeira)
Restaurante CABANA
CABANA restaurant
Restaurant CABANA

Hello Norma + Tanis –
I'm the youngest man on
the ship. Bent cripples
staggering everywhere –
7 Burials a day at sea –
Food 7/10 Cabin 6/10 –
wine ok – Enjoying the
break. *Now* what?
          Love Spike !

MD 218

N Farms. Tanis Dawn

Bayswater
London W2
ENGLAND

TO THE IDIOT
WHO'S GOING TO
SAY 'THERES A CAR
WAITING FOR YOU"
I KNOW, I ORDERED
IT! SO GO
AWAY CREEP.

Note on Spike's office door

COMIC ON STRIKE. No Jokes past this point.

Note on front door of no. 9 written when, according to Spike, 'Everyone else is on strike.'

As I'm working a
SIX day week - is it
possible not to book
me work on a Monday -
1 T need one day off -
badly

Don't knock me off
I'm trying to Save the
Whales
Spike Milligan

Note Spike put on his car whilst demonstrating in Trafalgar Square. You know what? They didn't.

To: Nick Curnow Esq.,
Phillips,
Edinburgh   *1st August, 1983*

Dear Nick,

   This is to confirm our telephone conversation that I will bid
£6,200 for 'IN THE MIRROR'.

   My contact will be my Manager, Norma Farnes, the late
Lady Calthorpe. Will you please contact her, she has Power of
Attorney over everything in my life except the Execution Squad.

                               Sincerely,

                               SPIKE MILLIGAN

MY OWN CAR is in
THE GARAGE. ITS GOT
A PARKING PERMIT ON
IT. WONT BE LONG.

Spike MILLIGAN

We're wasting our time darling —
we're going to pay the Lot.

A note I wrote and put on his car

15.5.78

WOULD YOU SIGN THIS
BOOK 'TO PAUL' THIS
BOY HAS HAD A COMPLETE
* BREAKDOWN AND LOST HIS
JOB AND WONT GO OUT
(£ LETTER ATTACHED EXPLAINS)

* Take him to a Garage

1) Richard ⌢ ²who _____ ?

He's methodical about filing. As I usually get the blame for losing things, whenever he borrows anything I make a note as proof – you can see it works!!

9.9. Scripts

Spike HAS Got No 2 Script.

Well I don't have it now

Deborah Rogers Ltd — Literary Agency

HITLER IN LIVERPOOL

by

John Antrobus

This man is a genius – and the fucking world is blind to it!

5–11 Mortimer Street, London W1N 7RH   Telephone: (01) 580 0604/5 Cables: Debrogers London W1

S. Milligan

(I mean Hitler of course)

(S)

ALL THE WORLD AND HIS WIFE
HAVE SIGNED COPIES OF "MONTY"
EXCEPT THE SCHLAPPER/MEMORY BANK/
DAMAGER ON THE GROUND FLOOR.

ITS NOT FOR:
  A) MY MOTHER
  B) MY FATHER
  C) MY FRIEND

ITS FOR ME — REMEMBER
ME — SO SIGN PLEASE

P.S. NO "GOOD LUCK" CRAP.

He signed, 'Keep taking the tablets.'

To: Alec Fyne Esq.,
Associated Television Limited
London W1   *4th April, 1977*

Dear Alec,

I don't often ask for work, because I don't need it, but I would like to be in the Muppet Show, because I would be good in it. I am certain the Muppet people would like me to be in it themselves.

If there is any reason they don't want me in it, please let me know what it is.

I do hope you will give this letter serious consideration.

Love, light and peace,

SPIKE MILLIGAN

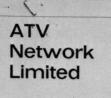

**ATV
Network
Limited**

a subsidiary of
Associated TeleVision Corporation Limited

ATV House
17 Great Cumberland Place
London W1A 1AG
telephone 01-262 8040

cables and telegrams
Ayteevee London W1
telex 23762

Registered Office:
ATV House
17 Great Cumberland Place
London W1A 1AG
Registered in England No. 874891

AF/RAA

5th April, 1977.

Dear Spike,

Thank you for your letter of the
4th instant and I will be in touch with the
Muppet people in Los Angeles in a day or two
and will see what I can do.

Kindest personal regards,

Yours sincerely,
A.T.V. NETWORK LTD.

ALEC FYNE
Casting Director

To: Alec Fyne Esq.   *25th July, 1977*

Dear Alec,

    Further to your letter of the 5th April, I would just like to know what's happening, obviously the Americans don't think I'm worthy of going on the Muppet Show.

    It's a sad day when English artists have to take second place to Americans.

    Do let me know.

                                        As ever,

                                        SPIKE MILLIGAN

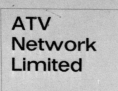

ATV
Network
Limited

a subsidiary of
Associated TeleVision Corporation Limited

ATV House
17 Great Cumberland Place
London W1A 1AG
telephone 01-262 8040

cables and telegrams
Ayteevee London W1
telex 23762

Registered Office:
ATV House
17 Great Cumberland Place
London W1A 1AG
Registered in England No. 874891

AF/RAA   18th July, 1977.

Dear Spike,

     I am sorry for the long delay in answering
your letter of July 25th but I have been away on
business and also on holiday and have only just
returned to the office.

     I have spoken to the Muppet people again
about you but unfortunately the show is booked with
the exception of two shows at the end of the year and
they are insisting on having a female performer. *

     However, they have now returned to America
until October and I will discuss the matter with them
upon their return.

        Kindest personal regards,

          Yours sincerely,
        A.T.V. NETWORK LTD.

          ALEC FYNE
        Casting Director

*Perhaps if I had the operation.

HEADLINE: Spike Milligan gives his all to
appear in Muppets show.

To: Alec Fyne Esq.   *24th August, 1977*

Dear Alec,

    Thanks for your letter regarding the Muppets. I see they only have two shows vacant at the end of the year, and insist on having female performers. Perhaps if I had the operation? Headline: SPIKE MILLIGAN GIVES HIS ALL FOR SMALL PART IN MUPPET SHOW.

                         Love, light and peace,

                        SPIKE MILLIGAN

Envoi. He gave his parts for other parts.
         Tell them all I bid them a fond farewell.

Two years later they rang to say, 'Would Spike like to do a Muppet Show?'

REMITTANCE		DATE OF PAYMENT	8 11 79

(handwritten) Ⓢ. JUST HAD TO SHOW YOU THIS LUNACY.

ITC ENTERTAINMENT LIMITED
ATV House, 17 Great Cumberland Place, London W1A 1AG
Telephone: 01-262 8040

PAYEE'S NAME AND ADDRESS

NORMA FARNES MGT

LONDON W2

ARTISTE'S NAME	PAYEE NO.	PROGRAMME TITLE
SPIKE MILLIGAN	02490/0093	MUPPETS 3 EPS65

PERFORMANCE DATE	NATURE OF PAYMENT	AMOUNT
WGER 120 EGER 10 AUS 6 SWIT 2		117.94
	Less: NATIONAL INSURANCE	
R	NET AMOUNT PAYABLE	£ 117.94

"R" INDICATES PAYMENT FOR A SECOND OR SUBSEQUENT RECORDING PREVIOUSLY TRANSMITTED

THESE FEES ETC. WILL BE NOTIFIED TO THE INLAND REVENUE. YOU SHOULD RETAIN THIS FORM CAREFULLY FOR FUTURE REFERENCE AS THE INFORMATION CAN ONLY BE REPRODUCED IN EXCEPTIONAL CIRCUMSTANCES.

Spike with the Muppets

To: Leslie E. Day Esq.,
Accountant,
ITC Entertainment Ltd   *28th November, 1979*

Dear Sir,

    I have a Remittance Advice Slip, and I would dearly love to know the meaning of the following, which is inscribed across the slip:–

          WGER 120 EGER 10 AUS 6 SWIT 2

I mean, is there any point in putting this on a piece of paper and sending it to me. If you think it is valid, then I can say:

          XOTP 3 LUW TXL 20. MIT 6 DPM.

    I will exchange the secret of my code, if you will tell me what yours means.

                    Sincerely,

                  SPIKE MILLIGAN

Directors

Lord Grade
Chairman and Managing Director

Jack Gill
Deputy Chairman

B. J. Kingham
Deputy Managing Director

E. S. Birk

Ian R. Jessel

David C. Withers

A. D. Brook

Secretary

Mr. L. Thompson

Cables: EYETECEE, LONDON
TICFILM, LONDON
Telex: 261807
Telephone: 01-262 8040

ATV HOUSE, 17 GREAT CUMBERLAND PLACE, LONDON W1A 1AG

Mr. Spike Milligan,

London W.2.

7.12.79.

Dear Mr. Milligan,

We were all completely flummoxed by your letter and were forced in desparation to call in our resident troubleshooter, a red-capped gnome of limited mental capacity.

After many uncomfortable hours pondering upon his shovel, he has admitted that your 'Q' is higher than his and is compelled to reveal the secret of the inscription:

West Germany 12%, East Germany 10%, Austria 6%, Switzerland 2%. All of which are percentages due under the Equity/Itv Agreement.

Distraught by his failure to decipher your code, he has demoted himself to Managing Director.

Yours sincerely,

Elizabeth Delborre
Overseas Residuals.

So he writes his interpretation to *Private Eye*:

To: Private Eye   *28th November, 1979*

Dear Sir,

On a payment slip from I.T.C. Entertainment Limited, I am given the following information.

WGER 120 EGER 10 AUS 6 SWIT 2

Is there any living creature, be it computer or otherwise, that could enlighten me on this code.

If I translate it, it would mean, Wagner is 120 years old, living on the Eiger, with 10 Australians, and six Swiss, all at the age of 2.

Sincerely,

SPIKE MILLIGAN

A postcard with photograph of British Airways 747.

Oct 27.

Hello Miss North Country
of 1949.
Guess what? they put me up
in a noisy motel - lonely -
however.. have now got
a house in the bush .
lonely, saw a Wallaby
on the lawn this morning
All in order. Weather
lonely . Day off to day -
alone - lots of showers -
classics on ABC Radio -
writing Vol III war memoirs
Love Spik

POST CARD

BRISBANE
2¢ Oct
1977
QLD 4000

AUSTRALIA BROKEN BAY
SENDERS ADDRESS
ON BACK OF ENVELO
25

Norma 'I'll never get married
again' Farnes

Bayswater
London
W2

UK

The British Airways 747,
powered by 4 Pratt & Whitney
JT9D-7 engines, designed and built
by the Boeing Airplane Company.

Printed in Great Britain

I keep chasing him to finish books.
When he's in this country it doesn't happen – when he's away, he tries to
ease my mind by putting on postcards that he's getting on with it.

37

Still trying to ease my mind – different book.

OLD MELBOURNE GAOL
This bluestone Gaol complex was
built 1841 - 62. Since then it has
sheltered more than 50,000 pris-
oners.
Model of Harry Power, the
bushranger.

NATIONAL TRUST OF
AUSTRALIA (VICTORIA)
Open for public inspection

NU-COLOR-VUE
OF
AUSTRALIA

NAT 6
NCV 2784

POST CARD

Dear Norma Tanis –
Melbourne went well –
back into the suitcase
and onto Tasmania –
I'm pressing on writing to
finish the book of
numerous poems – love to
all –
        Love Spel

Can u pass
enclosed PC to
Mike Haymes. Ta.

Easing my mind yet again – different book again.

I found quite Safari Ranch. Living in Rondavels
Zebra – Deer – Geese
Peacocks – roam the grounds.
Food 7/10 Wine 10/10 But
Quiet. Show going very well.
Warm days – Cold nights –
by day I'm writing Vol V
of War Memoirs – alas I dont
have the mass of ref books I
need. Love to Tann
Spike

POST CARD
POSKAART
RSA 20c

Miss N Farnes
Bayswater
London
W2
England

THE WARY AND THE WEARY
After a long day's hunting, the "King of Beasts" and his close companion watch smaller game from a tree-shaded hideout.
Southern Africa
DIE JAGTER EN DIE GEJAGTE
Na 'n lang dag in die jagveld hou die Koning van die Diere en sy maat die kleinwild uit 'n skaduryke skuilplek dop
Suidelike Afrika

No. 54
KΕΡΚΥΡΑ
CORFU'
CORFOU
CORFU
KORFU

Villa OK - ½ light bulbs
dead - car dodgy -
Low on water -
English crowd the
entire fringe of Island
(Aye oop! et) inland
quiet. Wine 10/10.
found a white Mateuse
weather starting into Autumn
but lovely - cool breeze

ΕΛΛΑΣ 12
HELLAS

Norma

Bayswater
London w2

ENGLAND

© Trimboli - Via Puccini, 67 Pescara (Italia)

FOTOTECHNICA ΑΦΟΙ ΚΟΚΚΑΛΗ ΚΕΡΚΥΡΑ - ΤΗΛ. 28-105

C o r f u

No comment.

Spike and the Press

To: The Editor,
New Scientist   *15th July, 1983*

Sir,

Your little snippet on the new 'Music on hold' during telephone calls; it is a continued extension, of course, of this appalling musical dysentery called Muzak. If ever there was a harbinger of George Orwell's Big Brother in 1984, this is it and chronologically he is not far out.

I have managed to equate the situation. In phoning Qantas I was put on to 'hold music' when I finally got through to the man, I said: 'Just a minute', I then sang him a whole chorus of Hey Jude, which seemed to baffle him entirely.

I tried to rationalise by explaining his Company had been kind enough to play me two choruses of some crappy music, and I was returning the compliment. If we all did this I think we might close down this pointless waste of energy.

Of course, the most meritorious level this new sound has, is the Super Loo. Without being crude, musicians' music being played in a shit-house. God what a proud day. I had heard of chamber music, but this is ridiculous.

Yours, wearing ear muffs, and
a switched off brain.

SPIKE MILLIGAN

THE BAY OF PLENTY TIMES

LARGEST PAID
CIRCULATION IN
THE BAY OF PLENTY
MEMBER NZ AUDIT
BUREAU OF
CIRCULATIONS

P.O. BOX 648 TAURANGA

TELEPHONE 83-059, CLASSIFIED 80-616

TAURANGA
MT MAUNGANUI
TE PUKE
Centre of the
Bay of Plenty

111th Year   24,955   THE BAY OF PLENTY TIMES, FRIDAY, NOVEMBER 26, 1982   PRICE 20c

Improved weather raises rescue hopes

TIMARU — The weather in Mt Cook improved dramatically this morning, raising hopes that stranded climbers Phil Doole and Mark Inglis may be lifted off by helicopter round lunch time.

Helicopter pilot Ron Small was called from Tekapo and arrangments were made for a drop of supplies as soon as possible.

Winds at the snow-cave site of the two climbers near the summit of the mountain had dropped to about 40 knots — sufficient to allow the supply drop.

The sun was shining on the west side of the Main Divide and scenic flights there were operating.

This raised hopes at park headquarters that the weather might improve even further at the rescue site.

Winds would have to drop to about 15 knots for an airlift to be attempted.

In a radio link earlier the climbers said they were not suffering from severe exposure.

"They're now happy with the idea of a few creature comforts like more socks," Mt Cook chief ranger, Mr H.A. Youngman, said.

"We'll also send oxygen, antibiotics and another radio with batteries."

"The Spy who came in from the Cold", by Le Carre, was to be one of three books included in a drop bag. "Puckoon", by Spike Milligan and "The Ninja" (Eric van Lustbader) were the others.

"From what they've told us there are no serious medical problems," Dr Dick Price, of Oamaru, said.

Frostbite the men were suffering was not as serious as "tropical war type" gangrene, he said.

"But I'd like to see the extent of it," Dr Price said. I'd rather they didn't have frostbite."

He could only assess the severity when and if he joined the two trapped climbers.

(NZPA)

To: The Editor,
The Bay of Plenty Times
New Zealand   8th December, 1982

Dear Sir,

I hear that Phil Doole and Mark Inglis were trapped on the slopes of Mount Cook, and I was delighted to hear that among the supplies dropped to them was my book Puckoon. It was for this very reason that I had the book printed on rice paper, so that in case of stranded climbers it was edible. Chapter Four was extremely nourishing, as it had been printed with Soya Sauce. On the point of mountain climbing, I don't know why people are so mean, and don't take the bus.

Love, light and peace,

SPIKE MILLIGAN

P.S. When are the All Blacks coming here, life is very dull without them.

44

Dear Sir,

One thing has been missing in the Ceremonies concerned with Peter Sellers death, and it is one, I think, somebody should make comment about, and that is at no stage was there any attempt to introduce any connection with the Jewish side of his family. As his Mother was Jewish, most certainly then he was Jewish, whereas he did choose to be a Christian (though sometimes he fancied various other religions), his whole attitude and personality seemed to be that of a Jew.

Because of this I wish some small representation by the Jewish Synagogue could have been reported or mentioned during these Ceremonies.

There I feel better now.

Sincerely,

SPIKE MILLIGAN

My Dear Mr Milligan,

I read your letter in the "Jewish Chronicle". I do not understand what you mean by "at no stage was there any attempt to introduce any connection with the Jewish side of his family" - I too have wondered about this - after all a Jew does not usually have a funeral service in the Anglican church - you say that he chose to be a Christian" - I had read some time ago that his mother - of whom he was particularly attached to was a Jewess - this makes him a Jew - few people knew of his religion and obviously he did not find any pride in it - what a loss - - - his wife obviously did not think it mattered to him or else she would have spoken to a rabbi or even the Canon would have advised

2.

her properly - We jews get so much criticism that if our own - and such a talented man prefers not to recognize his people then what can be done?

You say "there I feel better now" - well I don't know if I feel better but I hope you do - .

Very Sincerely,
Esther Wilson

P.S. I am just watching clips of Peter Sellers films on Television what talent —

To: Mrs Esther Niren   *26th September, 1980*

Dear Mrs. Niren,

How nice of you to take the trouble to write. I am sorry you don't feel better about my letter, I think you should, as it is written by a Roman Catholic, which shows that he is concerned with the Jewish people, their tradition and their religion, which I think are among the most splendid in the world.

So, do not lose sight of the fact that at least Spike Milligan thinks the Jewish people are very very important.

It's a strange thing that in the Goon Show personnel the Goon Shows consisted of – two Jews, Peter Sellers, and Max Geldray, one Welshman, Harry Secombe, one Irishman, myself, a Roman Catholic, but no English. What would they do without us?

Love, light and peace,

SPIKE MILLIGAN

DAILY EXPRESS

SIR, I AM DELIGHTED TO SEE THAT MY CLOTHING IS IN THE SAME IMPOVERISHED STATE AS THE LEADER OF HER MAJESTY'S OPPOSITION. THE TRUTH IS MICHAEL FOOT AND I SHARE THE SAME PAIR OF TROUSERS. WHEN HE IS IN THE MOTHER OF PARLIAMENT SPEAKING IN THE STANDING POSITION, I AM IN MY BEDROOM NAKED FROM THE WAIST DOWN.

THE REASON WHY HE IS RARELY SEEN ON THE WEEKEND BECAUSE THAT'S WHEN IT'S MY TURN FOR THE RAGGED TROUSERS.

THE MUTUAL TROUSERS ARE A VICTIM OF THATCHERS MONETARISM WHICH STRIKES THE VICTIM FROM THE WAIST DOWN, THAT IS WHERE THE POCKET IS.

SINCERELY, S.M.

Opposite: Telling his friend Michael how to dress, with his shirt hanging out

To: 'The Old Codgers',
Daily Mirror   *18th May, 1981*

Sirs,

I have read the labels of various modern edible commodities, with all the crappy technical information on them which baffles the purchaser.

Can anybody tell me what this means? It's on a tin of golden syrup, and underneath is written this: Slightly Inverted Sugar.

Is it all a ploy to drive us all bloody mad? I have looked up every dictionary in the world to find out what 'Slightly Inverted Sugar' is. Please somebody help me.

Sincerely,

SPIKE MILLIGAN

Dear Sir,

Like many jazz lovers I was appalled to read in Peter Holt's column that the English Property Corporation (Ugh!) have asked the Westminster City Council for permission to demolish the Pizza on the Park.

Knowing how contemporary English bureaucrats and entrepreneurs have all the finesse of Attila the Hun, no doubt this site will end up as one of those appalling faceless offices.

I am just writing this letter to say how desperately sad a place London is becoming. People abroad are asking the following question: 'Is London a City or an office block?'

Merry Christmas to all your readers, except, of course, to the English Property Corporation and the Westminster City Council.

Sincerely,

SPIKE MILLIGAN

To: The Editor,
Daily Telegraph   9th December, 1982

Dear Sir,

Reference the picture of the Queen Mother admiring the Royal Smithfield Supreme Champion 'High Voltage'. (Tel. 9th December).

It is desperately sad to think that within 24 hours of winning this award, this delightful creature will be chopped up for steaks by an Oxford butcher.

One cannot help but feel sympathy with those people who demonstrated outside the Royal Show.

Yours,

SPIKE MILLIGAN

To: Letters Editor,
The Washington Post
USA   6th January, 1983

Dear Sir,

I read with alarm that Congress has granted N.A.S.A. a budget of $970 million for the year 1983 to search for life in outer space.

May I, on behalf of the millions of starving on this Planet, wish them all a Happy New Year.

Sincerely,

SPIKE MILLIGAN

Dear Sir,

Despite the massive publicity campaigns that the English banks insert in the daily papers, I notice an incredible indifference and shortcoming at advisory level. They are forever inducing young people and students etc. to take advantage of such and such a bank. However, I have a young 16-year-old daughter who opened an account, she has a reasonable amount of money in it, but at no stage did any of the members of this particular bank (National Westminster, Covent Garden), suggest that the money would gain interest, by opening a Deposit Account. The girl was totally ignorant of this until I informed her of it.

If you want more funny stories about banks; I once placed $100 in that bank which advertises 'Our Man on the Spot', The Chase Manhattan Bank. I had $100 in the account, and over the years it went down to $70, and I was waiting for this wonderful institution to write to me, and say we suggest you put your money on deposit, otherwise our annual bank charges will eventually eliminate your account.

With this in mind I wrote to them, and I worked out that by the year 2040, my current account would have been eaten up, by bank charges. I then asked the bank the leading question: 'What would happen to my account?', and they told me I would have gone into overdraft.

I suggest by that time, I would become their 'Man on the Spot'.

Yours cheerfully, but certainly not
enamoured of British Banking System.

SPIKE MILLIGAN

To: The Editor,
Daily Telegraph   *4th March, 1983*

Dear Sir,

I sympathise with J.M. Farmiloe and the difficulty of withdrawing a handkerchief from his trouser pocket whilst confined by a seat belt.

Here is a solution; before entering the car, the driver removes his trousers, he then fastens his seat belt, and places his trousers around his neck, with the legs dangling behind him, this leaves access to the pockets quite easily, and allows freedom to get the handkerchief, which will now lie on the left or right shoulder.

It is advisable, before leaving the car to re-don the trousers to avoid indecent exposure.

Sincerely,

SPIKE MILLIGAN
Seat belt sufferer

Spike Concerned

To: *Charles de Haes Esq.,*
World Wildlife Fund,
Switzerland   *2nd September, 1982*

Dear Charles,

I have just returned from Namibia after seeing the Namibia Desert Elephants, which alas are now down to 13, perhaps 14 in numbers.

I think that, as last year one of the bulls was shot by a tourist, with the connivance of a local resident, their situation is most precarious. I spoke to a local Game Ranger who didn't seem to think that anything special was being done to conserve them.

You possibly know that they are a unique species of Elephant, with longer legs than the normal ones, a wider spread of the toes to travel on the desert, and also much leaner in shape.

I think if the W.W.F. were to write to Mr. Botha the Prime Minister of South Africa, pointing out that basically the responsibility for these lay solely with South Africa, and could he bring about some kind of programme that they might be preserved.

Do let me know, dear Charles, if you can carry out this request, it's only the cost of a letter and a stamp, and of course, hope.

Love, light and peace,

SPIKE MILLIGAN

NEW ZEALAND ANTI-VIVISECTION SOCIETY INC.

WITHOUT FEAR WE STAND FOR THE RIGHTS OF ANIMALS

P.O. Box 2065, WELLINGTON

13 January 1983

Dear Spike

Once again it is almost time for World Day for Laboratory Animals.
This year our Society is participating in the MOBILISATION FOR
ANIMALS originating in U.S.A. and, as you know, is designed
to close down the four main primate research centres.

Last year you were kind enough to send us a message which
was read out in civic square during the speeches. Your message
was very well received by the public and I ask if you would be
kind enough to send us a short message to read out this year
also.

Thank you, Spike, for your work for animals.

Yours sincerely

Bette Overell
HON. SECRETARY

To: Ms Bette Overell,
New Zealand Anti-Vivisection Society Inc.,
New Zealand   27th January, 1983

Dear Bette,

Delighted to get your letter in the New Year. What is so good is that the movement for the cessation of this appalling trade is actually spreading around the world, and you are an outpost in the Pacific, and God knows we need people as far out as that.

Our numbers are small, but our hearts are good. I am sending you a small donation towards some kind of help, if I had a million I would send it to you.

Here is a message for you, to read or print.

Jesus started on his own, he had literally then the whole known world living in contradiction of his beliefs, among it the mighty Roman Empire, and even his own fellow Jews, yet this one man, with 12 others, changed the course of Society, merely on the strength of his beliefs, he had no television coverage, he had no money, what he had was, that which is the greatest sword of all, and that's truth. The New Zealand Anti-Vivisection Society Inc., has that sword, and therefore, nothing but good can come of its use.

The animals of the World are indeed our brothers and our sisters, the fact that we slaughter them, eat them and carry out abominable experiments is proof of the great degradation of human society, and if they are all wondering why they are all so morose, so tense almost in one way or another on some kind of valium, deep down it's their consciences which are creating the trauma, until they see the light of doing as Jesus said when the strong have devoured each other, the meek will inherit the earth.

We are trying, we and all of the likes of us are trying to get the strong to devour each other, let us hope we win.

Love, light and peace,

SPIKE MILLIGAN

59

Handing in a petition at Downing Street – such a haunted look (1978)

To: Covent Garden Community Association
                                    15th November, 1976

Dear All,

This is just to write and say I admire your consistent stand against the destruction of the Covent Garden area as a living entity. It's just distressing that we are actually having to force our elected officers to do our bidding, by *opposing* them. It makes nonsense of democracy however, the C.G.C.A. does exist as a fighting entity.

I am sending my renewal membership, and an autographed copy of a book you might like to use for a jumble sale.

Love, light and peace,

SPIKE MILLIGAN

To: Vice Admiral Sir Patrick Bayly,
Maritime Trust Limited   *14th June, 1979*

Dear Sir Patrick,

I was delighted to read that the Maritime Trust has won possession of H.M.S. Warrior.

I can't tell you how happy it made me to know that this splendid ship will now be an inheritance which generations can see. Imagine the year 2500 – the joy of some intelligent child to walk on board this ship and see how it was in all its finery.

I am sending £5 towards the assistance of the restoration.

Warmest regards,

SPIKE MILLIGAN

To: *Honorable Mark MacGuigan,*
Minister of External Affairs,
c/o Canada House   *11th November, 1980*

Dear Sir,

I just wish to add my weight to object against Canada's voting during the International Whaling Commission Moritorium on Whaling.

You know that Canada's vote made you the hatchet man of the sea.

Unfortunately there is no organisation which allows me to cast a deciding vote as to how many Canadian bureaucrats should be killed this year, because I have no compunction in saying if there was one, I would do so.

I beg you to start thinking like Christians, and go on from there.

Sincerely,

SPIKE MILLIGAN

P.S. There was a seal on the back of this envelope, sorry the fur isn't white.

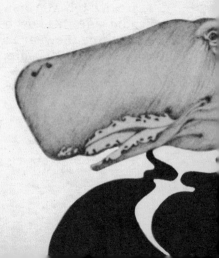

To: M.C. Mercer Esq.,
Director,
Fisheries Research Branch,
Resource Services Directorate,
Department of Fisheries & Oceans,
Canada   12th November, 1980

Dear Mr. Mercer,

I would just like to say how abhorrent I find you in casting the deciding vote at the International Whaling Commission Moritorium. Do you know this has made you the hatchet man of the sea?

Congratulations. One day someone will point at your grand-children and say to them – 'do you know your grandfather was the bureaucrat that exterminated a species?'

Love, light and peace,

SPIKE MILLIGAN

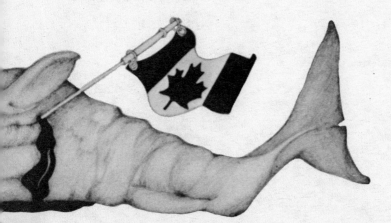

Dear Chief Constable,

I am writing to say how moved I was by the appearance of Detective Constable Alan Williams on television. To see a man so appallingly injured for life, and not to be in a state of rage and hatred shows a quality which most of us have lacking.

I think people take for granted the boys in blue, until something like this happens and then they all rush to their cheque books. What they don't know is even at this moment the lads in blue are going about their duty, and are in just as dangerous a position as Alan Williams was in at the time of the terrible incident, but it takes an incident like Alan Williams to draw attention to the fact that these boys are going around, most of them unarmed, in a country which is becoming increasingly violent.

I must say I have always had the greatest admiration for the British Police, and will always support them.

Would you like to pass on my warm regards to Alan Williams, and give him my best wishes, and tell him I have a feeling that Wales is going to win the Triple this year.

Most sincerely, and best wishes,

SPIKE MILLIGAN

GWENT CONSTABULARY

⌐ Spike Milligan, Esq.,   ¬

   London. W.2.

Police Headquarters,
Croesyceiliog,
CWMBRAN, Gwent.
NP44 2XJ.

Tel. No: Cwmbran 2011.
Telex: 498338.

J.E. Over, C.P.M.,
Chief Constable.

⌐   ⌐

All letters to be addressed to the Chief Constable.

Our Ref: CC/AW.   Telephone Ext.   Date   15:11:82.

Your Ref:

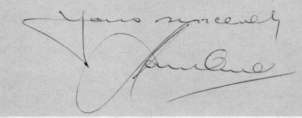

Dear Spike.

    How very kind of you to write to me. I shall
have great pleasure in passing on your letter to Alan
Williams.

    It has been very comforting to us all to know just
how much many members of the public support us even in
these difficult times when the police are under considerable
attack.

    You will be interested to know that Alan is making
great progress although psychologically it is going to be
an uphill struggle for him and his family.

    I am sure that if you are ever in the area he would
be very pleased to see you.

Yours sincerely

To: Lord Justice Lawton,
Royal Courts of Justice   *18th March, 1982*

Dear Lord Justice Lawton,

    It was with a great degree of satisfaction that I read your attitude towards pornography. God knows for the last 20 years we have suffered this appalling increase in this degrading trade, and I am delighted to see an upturn in the law.

    Congratulations.

Sincerely,

SPIKE MILLIGAN

To: Michael Wates Esq.,
Chairman,
Wates Limited   *25th May, 1982*

Dear Sir,

    I would just like to congratulate you on your restoration of the Bank of Scotland.

    I went to view it, and it is a sheer delight. Congratulations.

Love, light and peace,

SPIKE MILLIGAN

Dear Graham,

Thank you for your letter, yes the fight goes on. Basically, my dear Graham, this is how the nigger in the woodpile works; a new continent is discovered, people start to colonise it, and originally they are almost totally self sufficient. That means the financial structure of the country is controlled by its entity, i.e. they don't import or export. What happens is the big boys move in and see that there is a market overseas for, shall we say, wood and sheep. Whereas there are sufficient sheep to cover the home grown needs, and sufficient timber for home grown needs, there are, of course, owners who realise that they can export to overseas countries.

The native work force is too small to build up a business to a giant enterprise, therefore, immigrant labour comes in, on top of that, there's no population control; so here you have an eroding away of forests, basically for the big companies to make profits, but also claiming that they are 'getting jobs for people'. As population increases, the home demand increases for these people living in Australia, so, therefore, you have a two fold exploitation of the system.

The increase in domestic cattle, for export and home grown reasons, and the exporting of timber for the same reason, all the while the countries to which timber and meat is being exported, are also increasing in population, so the destruction rate of the home forests, and the increase of the grazing areas, naturally follows. If a country to whom goods are being exported goes financially bankrupt, or over-close on the contract, people are thrown out of work, both the native Australians, and the imported foreign workers. A cry goes up, two fold, the ecologists say we are gradually destroying our forests, and over grazing our land.

The overall picture is as world population increases, the demands for the goods being exported from Australia will increase, and as the Australian population increases, of course, the Capitalists are increasing their (a) wealth, and (b) the grip on the working force (bearing in mind, also that a large amount of the profits from the companies investing in Australia go to the parent companies in America, Japan and England etc.). They themselves start to import goods which are not essential, luxury goods, which develop into sometimes giant combines, David Jones and Myers Imporium, and all the paraphernalia which is bought by native Australians. So, a system is set up which gets more and more involved, as more and more people are involved; so that each country in turn holds the Sword of Damocles over each other.

The stronger the commercial sword, the stronger the threat, that is, if they feel so inclined. The Arabs can turn a tap off in their oilfields, and close down Japan. Even at the moment, the Japanese manufacturers have been forbidden by the Arabs to deal with any Jewish companies, to a degree the Japanese toe the line.

This position has been brought about by Capitalism; industries that were basically dependent upon energy, which they cannot grow at home, and, of course, the ever increasing population made the demand for energy greater. It is the ultimate example of what strangleholds can be made by what is called International Trade, which does not just stop at finance. The farmers of America, Mid West, are almost dependant upon the Soviet demand for grain. Here is an example of where it's really at. The American farmers don't give a fuck for President Reagan, what he wants is the Russian Government to buy his product, despite the fact that they are training atomic weapons on each other. So, we see that whereas Russia, because of over population, can't feed itself, America because of vast areas of land which have been felled, American farmers provide food, not for the native Americans, but for their enemy, Russia.

All that I am pointing out is the destruction of the ecology, i.e. trees chopped down for grain which is not essential to the country that has chopped them down, and all the while the demand is from an increasing population, you can see what a convulsive complex of interchanges the world of commerce is in.

Today, if they had in the past been enlightened, Australia would have gone for as much self sufficiency as possible, a limited population, and a minimum import/export business, today that nation would be blessed with not being in the terrible crushing world of inflation, and in a world where *nobody* can control the fluctuation of money. I will say that again, *nobody* has been able to control the fluctuation of money.

I predicted in 1956 that the expanding economy as it was then, would one day topple over like the Dinosaur, it has done that; I predicted that money would become like water and find its own level, that has come true, but whereas money we cannot control, if Australia can put a brake on population and immigration and control its ecological and commercial life around that, within 100 years it will start to pay dividends.

Talking of immigrants, they must only want to leave their own country because conditions there have become impossible, these conditions were made by themselves, i.e. too many children, alas those very immigrants are coming into Australia bringing with them their reproductive rate, so that one day, if things go on as they are, Australians will be looking for some place to emigrate to, when that time comes, there will be no more great lands like Canada, and America and Australia and New Zealand to take the overspill. So, the message is control your numbers, I don't know whether anybody will ever listen to the words of a clown like myself, but all I have said, I prophesy will come true.

So, in the light of all this, my dear Graham, do consider putting in your future publications, part of this very important message.

As I speak, here in England, we have four million unemployed, which must affect the wives and children, so we have something like ten million affected, it means we have too many people and the industries employing them have closed down, however, the bosses have already got it banked in Switzerland, and are languishing on their yachts in the Mediterranean, waiting for the market to come good again.

I hope you are keeping up the fight against the lunacy of the Franklin River Dam – here again we have too many people, 3,000 odd unemployed, and because of that they are going to drown a giant area, which has been declared a natural wilderness by world organisations. If it goes ahead and the 3,000 are employed, they in turn will have children and grandchildren who will need jobs, and then, of course, it would be a good idea to employ them on another dam to keep them employed, and so on and so on, and at the top of it all we have world leaders who are doing absolutely nothing in their manifestos to implement population stabilisation, and better still de-population.

69

There has never been a speech by any world leaders regarding this, except, of course, by Mao Tse Tung, who told the Chinese people to have big families, and now the Chinese have finally got the message, but they had to reach 1,600,000 millions before they did, even as they were taking a census, another three millions were born, and they have realised, only by actually making it *illegal* to have more than two children, that the idiot population will ever be controlled. You must not ask people, you must order them.

So, we start the New Year, I hope what I have said will have some affect.

Love, light and peace,

SPIKE MILLIGAN

P.S. I am dictating this letter over the telephone, because I am in bed with flu, and Norma, my Manager has told me of your gift of the book and badge, and also that I have been made Hon. Life Member, believe me these sort of things are the staff of life to me, if somebody believes that I am worthy of being considered a true conservationist, then I feel I have made a small step, alas the steps ahead are so vast, I wonder if I can make them.

To: William Beaumont Esq.   17th February, 1982

Dear Bill,

Just to say how desperately sorry I was, like all the rest of
the rugby world, that you have had to hang up your boots. It was
a shame just when I suppose you were at the peak of your
playing career, but we have to face facts, and you can still enjoy
coaching and watching the game.

I am glad that they have brought back Dusty Hare, I really
didn't dig Marcus Rose, he made two glaring mistakes in his last
two games, the previous one, there was a try on, if he had just
passed out to his flank, but he didn't.

Anyhow, glad Dusty's back in.

Looking forward to Saturday games, and being Irish I am
looking forward to Ireland winning the Triple this year.

Love, light and peace,

SPIKE MILLIGAN

GalleyWood House Aimes Green Waltham Abbey Essex Nazeing 2106

Spike Milligan,

London, W.2   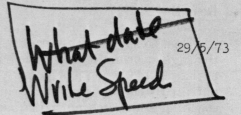 29/5/73

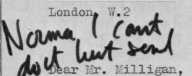

Dear Mr. Milligan,

Many thanks for your letter of May 17th.

Unfortunately, our 'Save Epping Forest ' rally
had to be postponed due to an Essex epidemic of
horse 'flu.

However, it does afford the opportunity of
extending another invitation to you to speak at
our meeting on Sunday July 1st.

It promises to be a massive protest involving at
least three hundred horse riders.   Other speakers
are George Sewell, who lives locally, Percy Bell
Chairman of the G.LC. and Lady Dartmouth.

.If you are unable to make the new date perhaps
you may like to send a message of support.   It
does seem absurd to choose 'plant a tree year' to
build an eight lane motorway through the last great
natural forest near London.

Best wishes,

John Gorman
Upshire Preservation Society

To: John Gorman Esq.,
Upshire Preservation Society,
Essex   *18th June, 1973*

Dear John,

    Alas, I cannot attend on July 1st but I am sending you a telegram offering my moral support to be read on the occasion. It will read:

'I think that I shall never see,
a poem as lovely as a tree,
that is if some bastard does not chop it down.

I support your fight to save Epping Forest.

    Signed: Spike Milligan and 20 dogs.'

                                    Sincerely,

                              SPIKE MILLIGAN

← Keep it in the family.

David C Deeson FInstD MIPR MBIMA Associate BAIE
AFL Deeson MA PhD DSc FInstD FISTC MIPR MAIE MBIM
Linda A Deeson   Pamela Deeson
Christina A Springham

pulse communications limited

Registered number: 1080349 England
Registered Office:
151 Dulwich Road London SE24 0NF   01-733 6201/4
Telex 916317 Deesonpress Ldn

Phoned. on ⑤ Return.

7 November 1977

*No — while the Catholics
include b. control — I'm not
wasting money on our*

Dear Spike

Catholic Fund for Overseas Development

Yes or No.

Would you be willing, please, to be publicly
associated with the work of the above charity?

*people who
give birth to
poverty —
better they
die*

Throughout the Third World millions endure
continual poverty - a poverty so grinding from
our point of view to seem unendurable, a poverty
that attacks the mind, the body, even the spirit.
But most struggle on throughout their short lives,
battling against impossible odds.

The Catholic Fund for Overseas Development - or
CAFOD as it is more commonly known - was founded
by the Bishops of England and Wales to help these
poor people - our brothers and sisters in Christ.
Not by hand-outs but by providing support for
constructive projects in which they can partici-
pate and which will permanently alter the conditions in which poverty and misery presently
flourishes.

CAFOD is already supporting hundreds of projects;
it could support many more if it had the funds
available.

To this end, we regularly place advertisements
in the Catholic press on behalf of our client,
appealing for assistance.

Would you allow us to write one or two advertisements 'around' a photograph of yourself and
thereby assist this very worthwhile cause?

A wholly owned subsidiary of The AFL Deeson Partnership Ltd

Naturally, all material prepared would be
submitted to you for approval, and there is
absolutely no question of anything appearing
in print without full clearance having been
obtained from you.

I look forward to receiving your reply.

Yours sincerely

David C Deeson   dcd:cas

To: *David C. Deeson Esq.,*
Pulse Communications Limited   *8th December, 1977*

Dear David,

Thank you for your letter which, of course, I read with that awful
pang that hits one when one reads of the insufferable conditions of
human beings. Now there is an old adage David, 'you have to be cruel
to be kind'. I have to ignore your plea for those very reasons, and that is
the Catholic Religion's failure to institute birth control within the
Catholic dogma. The present policy is sheer insanity and cruel in that
starving people give birth to more starving people and in no way has,
will and can the Catholic Church ever solve it by charitable collections.

If the Catholic See had their heads screwed on and included a
portion of its charitable monies to prevent the birth of starving babies,
I would do my damndest to assist them financially, but I cannot
support a policy which only maintains the level of poverty and
sustenance to continue further poverty by the birth of unwanted
mouths to feed. Believe me, a letter like this is very painful for me to
write. But, as Hamlet said, 'a good idea must give way to a better one'.

There was a time when I refused to help Oxfam because they
laughed at me when I said, 'in every loaf of bread put a prophylactic'.
However, as time went by they saw the logic in my reasoning and have
now set aside a portion of their funds towards birth control. I do hope
you will understand.

Love, light and peace, *SPIKE MILLIGAN*

75

To: R.G. Brooke Esq.,
Chief Executive & Town Clerk,
West Yorkshire County Council   *27th May, 1982*

Dear Sir,

May I commend the West Yorkshire County Council in their move to demand an Inquiry into the death of Helen Smith.

All in all, up to the present moment, the Judiciary come out of this in a very unsavoury light.

I, as an ordinary layman, having seen a photograph of the girl, not by any yardstick can I imagine that the bruises on her face and body were brought about by falling from a balcony.

I hope you all succeed in your very fine endeavour to bring justice to light.

Sincerely,

SPIKE MILLIGAN

WEST YORKSHIRE
Metropolitan County Council

DEPARTMENT OF CHIEF EXECUTIVE AND CLERK
County Hall
Wakefield WF1 2QW

Telephone: Wakefield 367111
R. G. Brooke — Chief Executive and Clerk

My reference: RGB/MHH   Your reference: Date: 2nd June 1982

Dear Mr Milligan

You are used to getting fan letters, but I am not. Thank you
very much then for your letter of support on the Helen Smith
case.

All Parties on the County Council feel extremely unhappy at what
has happened in this case so far. Although the County Council
wished to see an inquest into the death of Helen Smith, the
decision of the Courts means that it must now accept that the
Coroner has no power to hold such an inquest. It is probably
also fair to say that a Coroner's inquest would not be the best
means of getting at the truth, since the Coroner would have no
power to compel the attendance of witnesses beyond his
jurisdiction - which is where most of the witnesses in this
case are. The County Council therefore believes that the only
way of getting to the bottom of this sad case is for a full
investigation by the Attorney-General, who seems to be the
officer best able to undertake it.

I have drawn the attention of the Leader of the Council to your
letter. He does appreciate your support. Thank you for writing.

Yours sincerely

Rodney Brooke

Chief Executive and Clerk

To: G.G. Datsun Esq.,
Town Clerk,
Cambridge City Council   *15th April, 1982*

Dear Sir,

It has been reported to me that there is a circus, Sir Robert Fosset, to be allowed to perform in the precincts of Cambridge, in which there are wild animals. The lady from Cambridge, Miss Pamela Collins, phoned me up and told me that according to her, the Cambridge City Council had banned any live circuses in the area.

If this is true, I wonder if you can take the requisite action.

Sincerely,

SPIKE MILLIGAN

Spike and the Medical Profession

To: Dr I. Jordan   *21st August, 1967*

Dear Dr Jordan,

   I did want an X-ray for my stomach to verify any stomach
cancer present. You sent me to Sir Ralph Marnham, who looked
up my posterior. Now this is quite obviously to check for Cancer
of the Rectum, which I know I have not got.

   Can you please arrange for me to have an X-ray of my
stomach for Cancer?

   I don't want to go to another Specialist because that will
cost me another 5 gns. I just want an X-ray straight forward.

   Can you arrange it for me?

                                        Sincerely,

                                        SPIKE MILLIGAN

To: Ray Mole Esq., LHA,
Chief Executive Officer,
The Royal Masonic Hospital   14th July, 1983

Dear Mr. Mole,

In an attempt to improve the quality of life in your hospital, may I recount the following experience. The first thing I noticed was the appalling noise from the television sets which blared out from every ward-room, which I found totally unbearable, and I suggest that television sets should be fitted with earphones for the patients in need of peace and tranquillity, as in my case, and they should be able to get it.

Secondly, during the last war a well known torture, by the Gestapo was to wake a tired person up every hour, and ask them their name. I had an operation on my eye for a new lens; in the course of most operations one's systolic blood pressure goes down to about 100, this is in no way dangerous or low, except in major heart surgery, which I did not undergo. Because somebody *thought* my blood pressure was dangerously low, I was wakened up every hour during the post operative period, so much so, I thought I was going to have a nervous breakdown, and in a semi-conscious state I had to shout out to the nurse, unless she stopped I would get out.

I am just pointing out these two issues to you so that the quality of life might be improved in your hospital. I assure you the facts I give you are correct, and not fancied.

Sincerely,

SPIKE MILLIGAN

P.S. Likewise, if it is of interest to you, I was given a number on a wrist label; much later on an entirely different nurse came in, and said your number is . . . . and gave me a completely different number, I had to correct her, otherwise I might have had my right leg off.

A reply came from a Tony Prescott which did nothing to appease Spike:

To: Ray Mole Esq. LHA   21st July, 1983

Dear Mr. Mole,

I wrote you a letter on the 14th July, but got a reply from a Tony Prescott, who I have never heard of, and who makes no mention in his signature as to what his terms of reference are.

I would like some opinion, at your level, as to whether you think noise in a hospital is unnecessary; and the waking up of patients, when it was not necessary. I thought I might get some emotional response, like 'Yes Spike, television can be noisy, and nurses do get too efficient'.

The point is I have to have yet another eye operation, and I should hate to have to come back and endure the same situation at the Royal Masonic Hospital. That is why I am asking you whether my letter has been taken at a serious level, and that I hear the results of 'your letter will be noted and discussed with the people concerned'.

I originally did specifically ask for a quiet ward, as you can see by my letter this was literally ignored. I would like to know if you take any action, and please let me know the results, upon it depends on whether I use the Hospital again.

All else at the Hospital was very very good indeed, I am just pointing out two lunatic situations, which no hospital should tolerate.

I am writing to you again, because the letter from Tony Prescott seemed a bit vague, in as much as I do not know whether you dictated it, or you had any communication with him about it.

Please do let me know; I am journeying to South Africa on the 15th August, 1983.

Yours, most well intentioned,

SPIKE MILLIGAN

Note at bottom of doctor's bill:

'These accounts are prepared by microcomputer and the system can only function accurately if your cheque exactly matches the total fee shown. If in doubt please contact Fiona.'!

To: Dr Martin Scurr   *24th February, 1982*

Dear Martin,

Reference the note at the bottom of your bill. Please note that this bill is paid by a computer called Spike Milligan, and unless the figures on this cheque tally with the amount, two things will happen:

a) you have overcharged me.

b) or he has overpaid you, either of these will do for you.

However, if option (c) occurs, that is you have undercharged me, and (d) I pay the under-charge, it's three points to me and my computer.

Sincerely,

SPIKE MILLIGAN

P.S. I saw a human being today.

To: John Watling Esq., LDS,
Wimpole Street   *17th November, 1982*

Dear John,

For God's sake don't try and sell my daughter an electric toothbrush, she can't even afford a hand held one, and she's so silly she's liable to say yes if you sold her 400, and in the end the bill would come to me.

So, desist I say, or I will bring to bear on your private aircraft anti-aircraft fire of the most formidable nature not heard of since the terrible flak guns around Berlin in 1943.

I know I am due for a check up with you, but for Christ sake, I am doing a tour round the country of my One Man Show which involves me getting home at 3-00 a.m. on a Sunday morning each week, and unless you want to transfer your entire dental surgery on a Sunday afternoon you will have to wait until December when I return to London to open in the One Man Show.

Would you like two free tickets in exchange for an electric toothbrush.

> Love, light and peace, (especially to
> your last little crumpet who puts
> the bib around my neck).

SPIKE MILLIGAN

P.S. Have you managed to fly over any Beaujolais Nouveau.

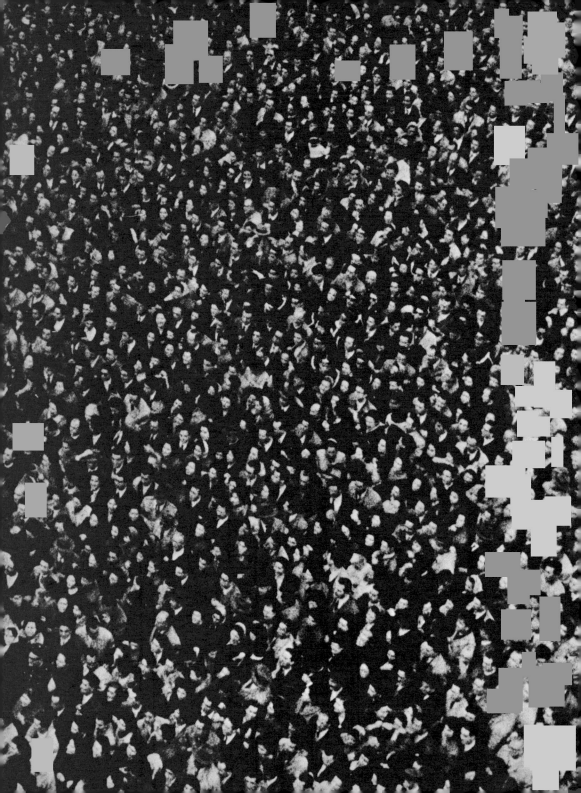

Spike on Population

To: Nicholas Guppy Esq.   2nd December, 1982

Dear Nicholas,

Re your letter of the 25th November, and the appeal. I am sending you £25.00.

A comment, on the world situation regarding all pressurised animals and people. All our causes will come to nought unless we have a parallel de-population programme world wide. China has got the message, but too bloody late. Even as they were taking the Census, three million Chinese were being born, making the Census out of date before it had been completed.

Do heed what I say.

Sincerely,

SPIKE MILLIGAN

Sir,

Whereas I am a member of the World Wildlife Fund, I notice in their advertisement in *Time* (27th December), they are mourning the world of the destruction of forests and warning against the consequences, which they put down to 'man's greed'. It makes it sound as though it's the work of Capitalists, and in the main it is, but it is the demand from a growing population which makes it all possible. Capitalists can't sell goods to people who are not there.

No, the real nub of the problem is over population. Reduce our numbers, you reduce the demands and the withdrawal of the Capitalists in expanding areas of commerce.

Running parallel with that advert is another piece of evidence showing how growth of population is even being catered for in advance. Page 53, Medicine, we have a gentleman creating gene miracles by making a giant mouse, and the ultimate reason is 'if we can make bigger mice, we can make bigger cows'. Might I say, bigger cows will eat more grass, and more grass means chopping down trees.

At the same time on page 11, we have James P. Grant, of the United Nations Children's Fund saying 'To allow 40,000 children to die like this every day is unconscionable in a world which mastered the means of preventing it'.

I have given three examples, three sets of people all meaning well; but getting nowhere.

When, Oh God, when will somebody at the top say to World Population stop, we need breathing space, stop enough is enough. Either the world depopulates (and I don't mean just the third world) or all these well intentioned gentleman's causes will come to nought.

At the present moment, as Alice in Wonderland said: 'It's all very puzzling.'

Sincerely, *SPIKE MILLIGAN*

Dear Ron,

In Action for Environment Newsletter, No. 99, I see your poetic heart warming message to the members.

As you know I am a total environmentalist, but I am one with a prophetic vision and I realise the strenuous efforts by people to retain an environment that they like. I notice that by sheer pressure of numbers some of our desired conservation programmes just *have* to give way under pressure of population; and this is most important, the *consumer* demands of the population.

When a factory expands it's not expanding for the fun of filling up the landscape, it expands because the people, and that is you and I, are increasing our demands for their products. Hence, battery chicken farming, and possibly eventually all farming will be on a battery system. I have sat next to intense environmentalists, with their wives, and six children, who have complained about the increased traffic on the roads, ignoring the fact that apart from him having a car, his wife has a second car, and three of his grown up children have cars, and yet he is in the forefront of the fight to stop widening a road to ease traffic congestion.

Therefore, my dear Ron, unless the environmentalists run a parallel population control programme they are all wasting their time.

I have repeatedly written to Action for Environment asking them to print my letters on this subject, but none have ever been printed.

Therefore, my enthusiasm for these people has diminished considerably.

I wish you well.

Love, light and peace,

SPIKE MILLIGAN

To: *Natural History Society*
South Australia   *13th January, 1983*

Dear Friends,

Find enclosed small contribution towards the cause. Thank you for the regular receipt of the magazine.

I would like to stress the point concerning the conservation of flora and fauna. I notice, despite all the good intentions of conservation bodies, very few are lobbying for the focal point which causes the destruction of animal and forest habitat, that is POPULATION. In 1936 the population of Australia was four millions – 45 years later it's heading for 20 millions. Unless a brake is put on it nothing but nothing can stop the destruction of the environment. At the present moment areas which have been set aside as National Parks etc. are only temporary holding areas, eventually the sheer tide of human numbers will overwhelm it.

Even as I speak, Snowdonia one of the National Parks here in England has had to be closed down because of tourist erosion. So, do consider in your future programmes and planning some thought for population stabilisation at a certain level. When you consider that the Woodchip Industry in Australia is not done for the natives of that country, but exported to Japan – what happens when one day the native Australians need the very timber that they have exported. Self sufficiency would be one of the most magnificent goals to aim for. The Aborigines did it since the dawn of time, and survived until the coming of the white man.

Anyhow, Happy New Year to you all.

Love, light and peace,

SPIKE MILLIGAN

To: Animal Aid   *8th March, 1983*

Dear All,

I cannot agree more with Sean Gallagher (Outrage No. 25). The pressure on the animal world increases in proportion with population explosion. If people are genuinely sincere about reducing this pressure they should keep their numbers down. I often see well meaning Animal Aid members, demonstrating with five or six of their own children, and each one of them will procreate again, and they can only live off the earth's surface and its produce.

One has only to look at India where 4/5ths of the people live near the breadline.

Sincerely,

SPIKE MILLIGAN

To: John Hayward Esq.,
County Cork   14th April, 1982

Dear John,

    Thank you for your letter of the 1st April, it was good to have a detailed breakdown of what exactly is going on out there. Of course, as you know the main nigger in the woodpile when it comes to conservation is man himself; and this is two fold (1) excesses of the affluent society, tins, bottles, oil slicks, which have reached momentus proportions is the nub of the matter, we are definitely over populated.

    Do you know that the Hunter-Gatherers of 2000 B.C. never knew hunger because of the prolificacy of the game, and the minimum numbers he was in, and to this day the Kalahari Bushmen have never known hunger on the scale, for instance, that the people of India know, or in Somali or Ethiopia.

    I say this because I am a Catholic, and I am desperately concerned that we should not continue to reproduce at the appalling rate we are doing. Eventually it will break down our standard of living, alas it already has. However, we have to keep fighting as I do.

    Give my love to everyone concerned.

                                          Love, light and peace,

                                          SPIKE MILLIGAN

Dear Eric,

Can you tell me if any of the organisations who have been carrying out birth control projects throughout the world have had any effect upon reducing, and I repeat, reducing population growth.

The leading question – can you name a country whereby the birth control people have had any major effect upon the birth rate?

I myself personally feel that these well intentioned people going around villages on bicycles and giving out contraceptives and little talks are overtly a waste of time. I am writing this letter to you because I have failed to get through on the telephone.

This is all leading up to me eventually trying to get our Government interested in taking *positive* steps. A simple one would be to give the equivalent of a child allowance for not having a third child. It may make for larger amounts of money from the Exchequer, but the benefits that would be reaped would be inestimable.

Also, I read that something like 20,000 immigrants have been allowed into England this year – with three million unemployed, don't you think this is lunacy?

As ever,

SPIKE MILLIGAN

To: HRH The Duke of Edinburgh, KG, KT,
Buckingham Palace   *7th June, 1982*

I was delighted to read in the *Telegraph* of your speech at Salford University. It is expedient when people like yourself talk in terms of 'the next 20 or 30 years are all we have to put the world on course environmentally'. I have been in touch with Charles de Haes in Switzerland and when he comes over here I am having dinner with him, and needless to say the topic of conversation will be de-population.

Alas, whereas there is a small nuclei of people like yourself, who are preaching the Gospel of population establishment, I can't help feeling that we are a small voice in the wilderness, and the nub of the matter is this:– unless population stabilisation is programmed by Governments, all our talk and all our efforts through Family Planning International, and Population Concern are really not having the effect that we require.

Yes, I know that the IUCN meeting in New Zealand did raise the question of population for the first time, but as I say, it has got to come as a Governmental dictum, and be included in all Government Manifestoes.

I myself am pressing as hard as I can by lobbying at the House. There does seem to be a small easing in the situation, but as you say, unless in the next 20 or 30 years a Government plan is not put into operation, like you say, it's goodbye to the animal world.

No need to answer, as I know you are busy.

Hope your boy in the Falklands is O.K.

Love, light and peace,

SPIKE MILLIGAN

To: *National Wildlife Federation,*
Washington DC
USA   *13th January, 1982*

Dear Sir,

In Issue 6, Vol. 11, I was pretty horrified to read Mr Norman Myers advocating that wild animals should be cultivated and then killed for human consumption; for the last 20 years I have realised that there is no hope in Hell of any substantial numbers of wild animals being in existence by the year 2500, except those, of course, which are kept now for the sake of beautifying nature, but, as Mr Myers advocates, on a plate at dinner time. This man is one of the increasing crowd of 'scientific idiots' who are gradually eroding away that most important quality of all in man, sensitivity. Mr Myers has lost his for sure; but sensitive people are aware that eating creatures is not the be all and end all of life. *If* there was no alternative to meat, I might go along with him, but I have survived happily for ten years without killing another creature.

This laughingly called 'ecologist' doesn't really see that the nigger in the woodpile of ecology is population explosion. As long as this explosion continues men will start to seek outside the normal levels of protein. This is gradually happening without these 'scientists' noticing it – live dogs being sold in street markets in the Philippines, and Mr Norman Myers promotion of eating wild animals is only another version of it.

Sincerely yours,
the last human being on earth,

SPIKE MILLIGAN

To: Billy Connolly Esq.   9th July, 1982

Dear Billy,

Unable to see you after the show owing to a severe attack of haemorrhoids. I was outraged that a man like myself who has practical haemorrhoids was not cast in your role. I know for a fact, from your army records, that you have not got piles and, therefore, I would hope you would resign this role in place of a man who is perfectly suited for the part, with an electric hand Truss, knitted by Nuns from the Poor Clare Order.

I really enjoyed the evening.

Love, light and peace,

SPIKE MILLIGAN

To: Wilfred Josephs Esq.   9th November, 1982

Dear Wilfred,

Sheer pressure of work has made it difficult for me to:

a) invite you to dinner
b) come and see you
c) ask you for money.

I am still trying.

Love, light and peace,

SPIKE MILLIGAN

To: Sir Harry Secombe　　　　　　　　　*7th December, 1982*

Dear Harry,

　　There have been distant rumours that you are still alive. So, I have stopped having Requiem Mass said for you on Sundays.

　　Here comes the request. I suppose you know that the boys of the 19th Battery have never got over your explosive night at our Battery Reunion, and of course, the buggers are pestering me for your return.

　　If you feel so inclined, and are not appearing at the Surbo Co-Asian local Odeon, we would be delighted if you could come along, it's 14th May, 1983.

　　I hope you got the photograph I sent you, taken while you were alive.

Love, light and peace,

SPIKE MILLIGAN

P.S. Ireland 36.
　　　Wales   Nil.

Opposite: Trying to get their act together

To: *Frank Dunlop Esq.,*
Young Vic   *17th April, 1978*

Dear Frank,

In my driving initiative I have discovered it's you who wants to direct/produce/fuck up THE DAY THEY KIDNAPPED THE POPE. I had no idea that you were going to direct it, but for Andre Foder who told me.

Of course, the whole things is, Walter Jokel has given me to understand that he has the rights, and he asked me to appear in it next year. You say he doesn't have the rights, so it sounds like a great start to a magnificent 'The Day They Not Only Kidnapped the Pope they Confused Me'.

Anyhow, Norma will contact him and ask him tactfully, thus: 'You little Jewish creep, you have been lying to us', or some such tactful approach. He, being near to starvation might say he is the sole possessor of the Pope Kidnapped Script, and I will be hearing from his solicitors in the morning, if not the Pope personally, etc. etc. Like water this will all find its own level.

One important factor Frank, if the play looks like dying on its bloody feet, I am not given to going down with it, and I will add dialogue of my own to make it a financial viable property.

I remember Tristan Jelly Neck, talking with other actors during 'Oblomov', and saying I was a disgrace to the acting profession, well I have not seen or heard of him since. They do say he is a re-tread remodeller in a Bata Boot Factory in Batley – just wait until Equity hear about that.

Anyhow, I look forward to working with you, and that's only for starters.

Love, light and peace,

SPIKE MILLIGAN

BAM Theatre Company
Brooklyn Academy of Music
30 Lafayette Avenue
Brooklyn, N.Y. 11217
(212)636 4156
Cable: Acadmusic

Frank Dunlop
Director of the Company

Berenice Weiler
Administrative Director

April 22, 1978

Dear Spike:

Just got your letter. I have been talking to the New York
producers for months about you and said that if you did
the Pope play the author and producers must accept some
improvising.

So nobody will be surprised if we do the same thing as
Oblomov and do "Son of the Pope".

Sod what any other actors said! You were wonderful in
Oblomov.

In fact what I suggest is that if we do the play together,
maybe you and I could do the basic adaptation into English
and embellish it in rehearsals.

Hope that might suit you.

Love and best wishes and see you very soon in London.

Yours,

To: Benny Green Esq.   *14th October, 1982*

Dear Benny,

I have listened to every one of your series, up to the Wes Montgomery playing 'Rainy Day'.

I have an awful feeling about us. Why is it people of our genre, because we delight in yesteryear sounds, are called nostalgic freaks. They don't say that about people who listen to Beethoven, who died long before Cole Porter. I think the reason we go for that type of music, is today people write disposable songs.

Thanks for playing the right stuff to the right man.

Love, light and peace,

SPIKE MILLIGAN

To: Lord Olivier   *31st January, 1983*

Dear Larry,

I am sending you this so you can enjoy mangling it into a shapeless mess, and throw it in the dustbin.

There are very few of us to have inherited this hatred for wire hangers.

Happy New Year to you.

Love, light and peace,

SPIKE MILLIGAN
Patron St. of Wooden Hangers

The following telegram was sent after Spike had received his invitation to the Royal Wedding:

PRINCE CHARLES: BUCKINGHAM PALACE, LONDON SW1
THANKS FOR THE INVITATION BUT ITS NOT GOOD
ENOUGH, I WANT TO MARRY YOU:
AS EVER, SPIKE

To: Mike McGear Esq.   *22nd July, 1981*

Dear Mike,

Thanks for the new record. I haven't played it yet, my music centre is off centre, but I think you are too late, some swine in the past has written a thing 'God Save the Queen', which believe me is bi-sexual because when I was young they were singing 'God Save The King', who knows one day it might be 'God Save the Puff'.

I notice you don't have a telephone number, so I am forced to write this bloody letter.

If you come to London let me take you to dinner, but hurry my age is running out.

Love, light and peace,

SPIKE MILLIGAN

To: The Rt. Hon. Anthony
Greenwood, MP

Dear Anthony,   *11th December, 1968*

I was delighted to read in the Sun, December 10, that you
are taking steps to prevent wilful neglect of old buildings
(sometimes important) allowing them to get into a condition that
they are condemned as unfit for human habitation, and then, of
course, selling the land and building flats at a great profit.

I wrote a long time ago to Richard Crossman saying that
this was one of the major destroyers of British architecture, which
had it been maintained in good condition would not only be
habitable, but also a joy to look at.

Congratulations on doing something about it at last.

Alas, in Finchley the last beautiful building, called Brent
Lodge, which I fought desperately to save had been let go by
none other than the Local Council themselves, and when I
pointed out the merit of the building, and an estimate of £20,000
would put it in good order, their immediate reaction was to have
the building pulled down.

If your idea goes through this of course, will stop these
20th century vandals (and ha̲ ̲o ways about it I have never
met a Local Council wit̲ ̲ ̲ ̲ outlook) from pulling down
the last vestiges ̲ ̲ ̲ ̲ semblance of beauty.

Regards as ever,

SPIKE MILLIGAN

̲ ̲ ow you are busy; if

Memo to Spike from Eric Sykes after reading the first Book of
Letters:

RE *Your letter on page* 52

Dear Anthony (deceased)

Richard Grossman (deceased)

*For gods sake don't write
to me*

ES

Written to Sir Michael Edwardes when he received the £990m grant from the Government:

Dear Michael.

Lend us a quid. !

Regards

Spike (Milligan)

Dear Spike,

Attached. We got £990m or so — please bestow but don't ask for paying it back!

Michael.

To: Lord Grade   15th January, 1982

Dear Lew,

I, for one among thousands, am very very depressed at what has happened to you.

All Companies lose money at some time, and this is a case of rats leaving the ship not while it is sinking, but while it's having a bad time, and I have written to the newspapers and said so.

You have always had my heartfelt admiration.

Love, light and peace,

SPIKE MILLIGAN

P.S. You still owe me £25 from the gig at the Winter Gardens, Eastbourne, when you promised me a bonus.

To: Lord Delfont,
EMI Limited   10th December, 1979

Dear Bernard,

For God's sake don't leave Charles Marowitz and his Enterprise homeless. He is one of the vital people in the Theatre, even though he goes, in the main, unsung.

I know it's difficult but this man really deserves support. I am willing to pitch in at a Charity Concert if that would help.

Love, light and peace,

SPIKE MILLIGAN

To: Mrs Loretta Feldman   14th December, 1982

My dear Loretta,

    As you know words are bloody useless at a time like this,
but you know how I feel.

    When you come over, please see me.

    It was a terrible loss for me, God knows how much it was a
loss for you.

    He wasn't just a funny man, he was a bloody nice fellow. If
life is a game of cards, somebody is cheating.

                                                    Love,

                                                    SPIKE

Opposite: I always told Spike not to swear in front of Marty (June 1971)

COWAN BELLEW ASSOCIATES LIMITED

45 Poland Street, London W1V 4AU
Telephone: 01-434 3871/9
Answering service: 01-434 3871
Cables: Cowboy London W1
Telex: 919034 Namara G

4th January 1983

Dear **SPIKE!**

Sir Harry Secombe will be back from Barbados for a
Gala Night on Sunday, 16th January, at the new
Secombe Centre - the first theatre to be named after
him - in Cheam Road, Sutton, Surrey.

The evening starts at 7 with a "Secombe Sizzler" cocktail
and other diversions in the foyer.

Then, at 8, there's a performance of a new version of
"Dick Whittington" by John Ashton, directed by Glen
Walford, and afterwards a celebratory buffet supper
plus champagne.

It would be lovely (and a nice surprise for Sir Harry)
if you could be there among the special guests, and we
look forward to hearing from you as soon as possible so
that the appropriate arrangements can be made and
two guest tickets despatched to you in good time.

See you at The Secombe ?   Do hope so.

Best wishes.

Beau Nosh III

Ouc of la Garoupe.

To: Laurie Bellew Esq.,
Cowan Bellew Associates · 11th January, 1983

Dear Laurie,

　　Further to our telephone conversation, I have sent off the telemessage to Sir Harry, I do hope he gets it. Spike did want you to have a copy of the message, and it is:

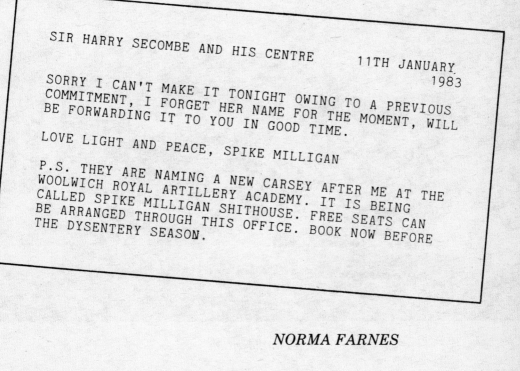

SIR HARRY SECOMBE AND HIS CENTRE　　　　11TH JANUARY 1983

SORRY I CAN'T MAKE IT TONIGHT OWING TO A PREVIOUS COMMITMENT, I FORGET HER NAME FOR THE MOMENT, WILL BE FORWARDING IT TO YOU IN GOOD TIME.

LOVE LIGHT AND PEACE, SPIKE MILLIGAN

P.S. THEY ARE NAMING A NEW CARSEY AFTER ME AT THE WOOLWICH ROYAL ARTILLERY ACADEMY. IT IS BEING CALLED SPIKE MILLIGAN SHITHOUSE. FREE SEATS CAN BE ARRANGED THROUGH THIS OFFICE. BOOK NOW BEFORE THE DYSENTERY SEASON.

NORMA FARNES

Two old friends

M
298111 PO PD G
TS15/102 LN

Y0021 ELB4593 EOF776 FIH517
GBXX CO AUWI 028
WIEN RA 28 05 1233

MR SPIKE MILLIGAN   BAYSWATER
LONDONW2

WHY DONT YOU SEND ME A TELEGRAM ASKING ME HOW I AM?
I AM FINE ARE YOU FINE
    VIENNA TOM

COL 9 LONDONW2

298111 PO PD G
TS15/102 LN

Peter's last telegram to Spike:

M.
298111 PO PD G
299992 PO TS G
N91 1212 LONDON T 65

MR SPIKE MILLIGAN
W2

DEAR SPIKE I AM DESPERATE TO HAVE SOME REAL FUN AGAIN WITH YOU AND
HARRY . PLEASE CAN WE GET TOGETHER AND WRITW SOME MORE GOON SHOWS ?
WE COULD PLACE THEM ANYWHERE I DONT WANT ANY MONEY I WILL WORK JUST
FOR THE SHEER JOY OF BEING WITH YOU BOTH AGAIN AS WE WERE .
LOVE
    PETER

COL 5 72 . ? WRITE SOME MORE .

299992 PO TS G
298111 PO PD G

31st July, 1980

Dear Spike —

I am afraid I sent my tiny tribute to The Times too late, but would like you to have it. Hope to see you soon.

Love from

B.

Spike Milligan Esq.

Until recently Sam Johnson's Obituary of David Garrick 'His death eclipsed the gaiety of nations and impoverished the stock of harmless human pleasure' seemed both artificial and overdone. Garrick's field of operation was so limited.

But in these confused and troubled times, when humour often seems the only prop to lean on, the death of Peter Sellers suddenly makes that epitaph spring to life in a way that millions of people must feel with a personal pang. The freedom and pure enjoyment of his interview with Parkinson, the authority and beautiful balance of speaking voice and the life in the eye, confirm what many of his colleagues always guessed, that buried away inside him was a great straight actor, probably even a great classical one, waiting perhaps until his middle sixties to make its appearance.

All this leaves out of account the break-up of the greatest comic triumvirate of the century. We have indeed suffered a cruel loss.

To: Lord Miles,
Mermaid Theatre   1st August, 1980

Dear Bernard,

   Thanks for your letter and the tribute, indeed the sound of
laughter has certainly been dulled, but it's one of the Arts that is
born of the Phoenix, and rises again and again.

                                    Love, light and peace,

                                    SPIKE MILLIGAN

Sir David Steel,
Chairman of the Mermaid Theatre Trust,
and Lord Miles

request the pleasure of the company of

Mr. *Spike Milligan*

in the Visitors' Gallery of the Stock Exchange
from 5.00 to 7.30 p.m. on Monday, 20th October,
for drinks.

Lord Miles will endeavour to amuse the Company
between 5.30 and 6.00 p.m.

Informal Dress   R.S.V.P. to
                                  Mermaid Theatre, Puddle Dock,
                                  Blackfriars, London. EC4V 3DB

*Dear Spike Do pop in y
In can. I'm sure youll enjoy
it. I'm collecting all my
famous friends to Decorate
the ocasion.*

Can I in a lift

Bernard

To: Lord Miles   *6th October, 1980*

I am sorry I will be cruising somewhere in the Balearics on that day, but give my love to those swines who are making money by sitting at the telephone letting other people squander theirs. Tell them that I hope during the proceedings, Jesus does not repeat his entry, and do what he did to the money lenders.

I wonder what Ladbrokes were quoting when Jesus was on the Cross – 'Would he go at 2-00 p.m. 3-00 p.m. or 4-00 p.m.' or would the thieves each side of him (who were 100 to 1 on) become the favourites.

The golden sand of time is running, and I haven't seen you for nearly two years. Yet we love each other; why then is this pernicious system in charge of us, and not the reverse?

My love to Lady Miles.

Love, light and peace,

SPIKE MILLIGAN

P.S. I notice that your name hasn't gone metric yet.

To: Herbert Kretzmer Esq.   *10th December, 1982*

Dear Herbie,

Getting a fan letter from a middle aged ex South African Jew, who was within inches of being able to kill Michael Foot and didn't, is indeed an uplifting experience in the world of literary correspondence.

But seriously folk (note the singular), my show doesn't really exist, it's a series of junk tied together with plain NERVE. I mean, if my jokes were teeth they would have been extracted 40 years ago.

However, I would like you to know, and a lot of critics don't, and accuse me of this, that all the jokes in the show were originally written by me, but alas other comics have done the rounds with them. If they go on doing the rounds with jokes I think my future is going to be on a milkround.

Anyhow we keep threatening to have dinner together, the threat on my part still remains. Make a threatening dinner phone call to me and you can rest assured that the message will never bloody well get through to me, primarily because my house is full of loving women.

Apparently the New Year is on its way and would you believe yet again the unimaginative bastards are going to call it January. Given the chance I would call it Thrallofick. Just think of heading your newspaper the 3rd of Thrallofick, 1983, what a difference it would make.

As Ellington said: 'Love you madly still'.

Why didn't you come round back stage after the show, I had prepared for your arrival by leaving as quickly as I could after the show – apparently my trap failed again.

Love, light and peace,

SPIKE MILLIGAN

To: Elton John Esq.   *1st May, 1981*

Dear Elton,

It has come to my ears that you think I am displeased with you. Well, it's all very confusing. I wrote around to a few of the pop luminaries trying to get £1,500 to save elephant families from being slaughtered, and transported to a game reserve where they would survive; and I wrote to you, the letter was sent to your address in Los Angeles, I got it from your London office as you were there at the time, the address I sent it to was – c/o. Rocket Records, 211 Beverley Drive, Suite 205, Los Angeles, 90212.

(a) I never received a reply from you, and (b) I never received a reply from whoever received the letter. If a creep who opened the letter didn't tell you she/he/it/shithead is responsible for my feelings towards you, because the least I expect of anybody is a reply to a letter. It's like when you turn a tap on you expect water. If you received my letter personally and didn't reply then my opinion of you is valid, but I have heard from Joan Thirkettle of ITN News that you said you never received a letter. This message was passed on to me by my Manager, Norma Farnes – let's all four, take our clothes off, join hands and play ring-a-ring-a nettles.

So, over to you to tell me where the truth lies. Personally I would much prefer you had sent £14,000 to Save the Elephant, and let somebody else pay £13,000 to buy the scripts. That way the world, for my money, would be better off.

However, it's not too late to send me £1,500 to save an elephant, you can name the elephant whatever you choose.

I think we should call it after the secretary who never sent you my letter, then you can buy a female elephant, and I will buy a male elephant and call it Hitler, and in the mating season we can go and watch Hitler fucking your secretary.

Apart from that all is well.

Love, light and peace, *SPIKE MILLIGAN*

WATFORD

ASSOCIATION FOOTBALL CLUB LTD

DIVISION III CHAMPIONS 1968/69

Members of the Football League   The Mid-week Football League

Chairman E H John
Manager G Taylor
General Manager/Secretary R E Rollitt, FAAI

REGISTERED OFFICE AND GROUND
VICARAGE ROAD WATFORD WD1 8ER
Telephone Watford 21759/24729
Registered Number 104194 ENGLAND

May 12th 1981.

Dear Spike,

Thanks for your letter. I'm completely unaware of the letter you sent me regarding saving elephants - and nobody connected with my office ever passed it on. Heds will role! To put matters right I am sending you a cheque and would like to name the elephant Betty (after my personal assistant) and if someone else could buy one called Nick Nolte we can watch Nick Nolte fuck Betty (she's mad about him).

Can I say that already (my life). He scripts have given cause for much hilarity unfortunately, the writers of 'Mrs Dale's Diary', 'Monty Python', and 'Emergency Ward 10', have been inundating me with scripts!!

2

Also, if the BBC ever let you loose on the
public again with Q6 and I'm not
touring or signing footballers - would love to
do something with you — I'll rephrase that —
Would love to do the show.

Glad to see you are well — saw you
on that horrible Wogan show. I'm not going
to buy a wig — just a nice set of Lady D.
and HRH dinner plates.

Love

Elton.

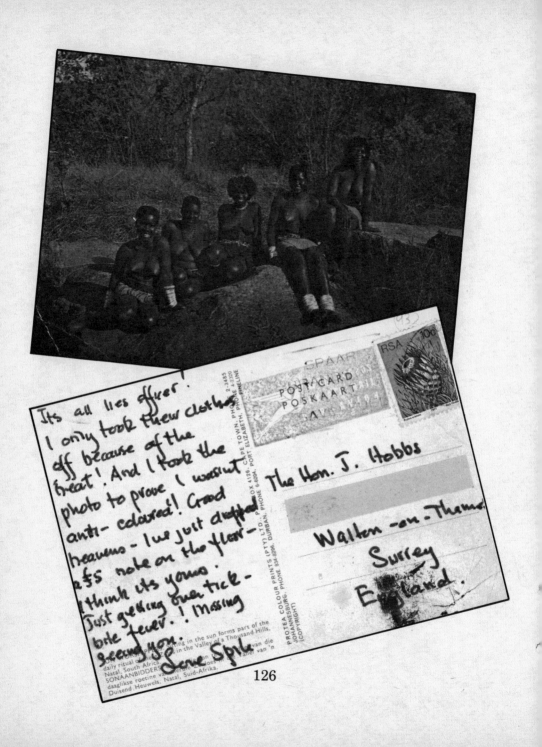

Its all lies oller!
I only took their clothes
off because of the
heat! And I took the
photo to prove I wasn't
anti-coloured! Good
heavens - I've just dropped
a £5 note on the floor -
I think its yours.
Just getting over tick-
bite fever. Missing
seeing you.
Love Spike

The Hon. J. Hobbs

Walton-on-Thames
Surrey
England.

Dear Jack of Walton —

This is the kitchen staff of the hotel I'm in. My room is the hut behind the girl pounding Army biscuits in a tube. I'm in bed with a 1020 temp — I did the show last night, with 101 — I went on for an encore at 1030 — tonight I'll try for 1040

Love Spike

AFRICAN GIRLS stamping and grinding maize which is their staple food. Natal, South Africa.
BANTOEMEISIES stamp en maal mielies, wat hul hoof-voedsel uitmaak. Natal, Suid-Afrika.

PROTEA COLOUR PRINTS (PTY) LTD., P.O. BOX 4126, CAPE TOWN, PHONE 2-3465
JOHANNESBURG, PHONE 834-8266, DURBAN, PHONE 6-6204, PORT ELIZABETH, PHONE 41-2320
(COPYRIGHT)

POST CARD
POSKAART

RSA 10c

Mr J. Hobbs of Walton

WALTON-ON-THAMES.
SURREY.
ENGLAND.

127

To: Cliff Morgan Esq.,
British Broadcasting Corporation   14th June, 1977

Dear Cliff,

    A belated congratulations on your O.B.E. I am sending you a Chinese Candle, which has no bearing on the honour conferred on you, but this will be the first time an Irishman has given a Welsh O.B.E. a Chinese Candle.

    Burn it at some dinner like party, and think of me when the Ruby shows through the glass.

Love, light and peace,

SPIKE MILLIGAN

Spike bored, waiting

To: Cliff Morgan Esq.   16th September, 1980

Dear Cliff,

Can I thank you very much for getting me two tickets to the last night of the Proms, but please tell Humphrey Burton he must wear evening dress on the last night of the Proms, otherwise I will never go to the pictures with him again.

It was a wonderful evening, but totally ruined by the music.

Love, light and peace,

SPIKE MILLIGAN

citement to come along (1976)

To: Mr & Mrs L. Drizen   12th July, 1982

Dear Mr & Mrs Drizen,

I have received your invitation to come on board the Silver Barracuda with some suspicion.

Question (A) Why is it only confined to aging clients of yours on whom you have placed large insurance premiums?

(B) Why is it that you two are going to be wearing emergency inflatable rubber life belts, while the guests have to have 80 lb. lead weights attached to their legs?

(C) Why has it been done under cover of darkness, with a strong outgoing tide, which I believe can float a body undetected out to sea without any chance of being observed?

All these things will have to be answered, my dear friends, before I step foot on a ship that has been condemned several times, may I say flying over a flag of convenience, i.e. W.C.

When Louis Tarlo has given me clearance of all these points, I will let you know whether I can attend.

Sincerely,

SPIKE MILLIGAN

Opposite: Twit

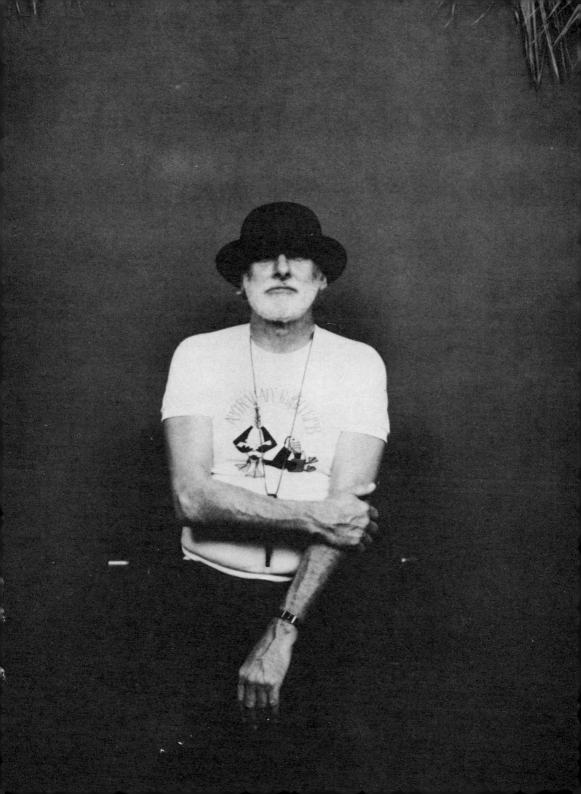

To: *Dick Douglas Boyd Esq.,*
Michael Joseph Limited   *2nd December, 1977*

Dear Dick,

Thank you so much for the leatherbound copy of Puckoon. How did you know that the colour I hate most is purple – the divine inspirational.

If I can have a choice in future, can I have black, or brown – or red to go with my bank balance.

As ever,

SPIKE MILLIGAN

MICHAEL JOSEPH LTD

52 Bedford Square London WC1B 3EF   Telephone: 01-637 0941 Telegrams: Emjaybuks London WC1
Registered in England No. 304786

Registered Office

6th December, 1977

RDB/CAL

Dear Spike,

My favourite leather is black shiny. I am sorry that you dont't like
purple. It cost us a hell of a lot of money because the binding is
made entirely of baboon bums and it is hard to find one large enough
to fit round anything but a paperback.

Tell you what, if we have a good year next year you'll get black. If
we're in the red you'll get red. O.K?

Yours,

To: *Dick Douglas Boyd Esq.*   *14th January, 1978*

Dear Dick,

Regarding being in the red or black – we are all going to be in the shit, so I suggest a brown cover.

As ever,

SPIKE MILLIGAN

The Book Bang (June 1971)

Spike Confused

To: Derek Mellor Esq., LLB,
Chief Executive & Town Clerk,
Leicester City Council

15th April, 1982

Dear Mr Mellor,

This is to congratulate you on your recent hunting ban.

It shows a great degree of enlightenment coming upon our people.

Sincerely,

SPIKE MILLIGAN

Leicester City Council

Chief Executive's Office
New Walk Centre, Welford Place, Leicester LE1 6ZG. Tel. (0533) 549922

Mr. Spike Milligan,

LONDON, W.2.

Derek Mellor LLB Solicitor
Chief Executive and Town Clerk

Our Ref	DM/MJP/GP/18
Your Ref	SM/NF
Please ask for	Mr. Mellor
Extension	6000
Date	20th April, 1982

Dear Mr. Milligan,

I was delighted as a "Goon-follower" of long standing (or, occasionally, other postures) to receive your letter of 15th April. We have a number of comedians serving on and working for this authority, but very few of your standard.

Unfortunately the City Council was not called upon to debate the fox-hunting issue; and even Leicestershire County Council, which did have such a debate, eventually decided not to ban the sport! I therefore wonder whether you really intended to write to us at all - but I'm very glad you did, as the rest of my post can be very boring!

Every good wish,

Yours sincerely,

Derek Mellor

To: Derek Mellor, Esq., LLB   *22nd April, 1982*

Dear Mr Mellor,

  Obviously the newspaper I buy deals in misinformation on a grand scale. I read in the Press that Leicester City Council had banned fox hunting, alas they were wrong, like fox hunting.

Sincerely,

SPIKE MILLIGAN

To: F.A. Wyeth Esq.,
Telephone House   7th March, 1978

Dear Sir,

On the evening of the 6th March, I reported my phone number at home, a 440 number, to the operator. This was on the 229 exchange, and the number I was speaking from was a 229 number. The Operator said 'I can't report it out of order now, as the Engineers are off duty, but I will report it in the morning'.

The following morning, that is 7th March, by 11-30 a.m. I still could not get through to the 440 number. I phoned the Engineers. I asked the Engineer had it been reported out of order, and he said 'No'. I then said, can you have it repaired and he said 'according to our card on the 7th February you reported your phone out of order, and when we went to repair it you said you didn't want it done' or words to that effect. I didn't know what it was exactly all about, but I repeated that the line is out of order, and could they repair it, and he then repeated the message, he had on this card of the 7th February, and I said 'I don't know what all this is about, I am reporting the line out of order, can you repair it', and then he said 'according to this card of the 7th February you don't want it repaired'. I then said 'What am I supposed to do', and then he said 'Well what do you want us to do'. I said 'I am asking you to repair the line, why are you making all these complications', he said 'we are not making any complications – do you want the line repaired', and then I said 'Yes, for God's sake yes, that's why I am phoning you', he then repeated the message about not wanting the phone repaired, and I said 'Can I speak to the Supervisor' and he said 'We are all the same rank here', and then I said 'I am totally baffled, what am I supposed to do now'. He then said 'do you want the line repaired', and I said 'Yes' and hung up.

I don't see why the subscriber should have to be cross questioned like this, and I resent it damnably. In the first place the Operator did not report it out of order, and he doesn't apologise for that, and starts to get at me about some technical details I don't understand at all.

I know it's totally pointless in trying to find out these faceless wonders, because (a) they don't give their names, and you will never find out who it is. I can't go along with this age of abstraction, because I'm a positive person.

Sincerely, *SPIKE MILLIGAN*

Some stopped
my clock — who
ever did — start it

SINCE NO ONE STOPPED
YOUR CLOCK — THE HOUR
CAME OFF G.M.T. I WAS
GOING TO PUT ON THE HOUR
BUT COULD NOT to FIND

THE WINDER .

Spike after opening a business letter and taking it home:

Dear Norma

Herewith — do what
ever has to be done

Love

Spike

To: *J.A.M. Kean Esq.,*
The Comptroller of Customs,
Private Bag,
Wellington,
New Zealand   *2nd September, 1977*

Dear Mr Kean,

I recently sent my friend, in New Zealand, a birthday present, it was a Bang & Olufsen Cartridge with stylus (for use on a record player). He wrote and told me that the Customs made him pay $21.00 on it. The article cost £16.10., so it does seem an outrageous amount to pay. Could you please verify that this was correct.

Sincerely,

SPIKE MILLIGAN

Mr J.A.M. Kean of New Zealand Customs replied asking for 'your friend's name and address and approximate date' and they would investigate.

To: *J.A. Kean Esq.*   *29th September, 1977*

Dear Mr Kean,

I was delighted by your prompt reply. I loved the head on your letter 'Private Bag', do you carry one around with you. Anyhow, it was jolly nice of you to reply, and offer some help in this case.

The story is, my mate, from World War 2, Harry Edgington, happened to mention to me that he couldn't hear the records I was sending him, because he was skint, i.e. broke, and the price of a new cartridge with stylus was a bit heavy on him, so I thought I would make a gift of one to him for his birthday, from England. When it arrived and he had to pay the total amount he would have had to pay in the first place, (a) he got a roasting from his wife, and (b) he had to borrow the money to pay the Customs duty, and I thought it added up to a very inhuman sad occasion.

Therefore, I am delighted by your offer of help.

Find enclosed present from me, for being a good boy.

Love, light and peace,

SPIKE MILLIGAN

P.S. His name is Harry Edgington Esq., Wadestown, Wellington. Left England, 25th July, 1977 so say, about 1st/2nd August, 1977.

143

24th June, 1980

To: David Jackson Esq.,
Interphones Limited

Dear Mr Jackson,

There seems to be some kind of misunderstanding about exactly what I wanted done to my interphones, by the young engineer who attended today, 24th June, so, therefore, I will spell it out to you.

When the phones were first installed, if one subscriber pressed the button to another subscriber, in another room, one could hear it buzz, at the other end and this intimated at least it was buzzing.

Recently after a visit from one of your men last Friday, who I wanted to rectify this, it still does not buzz at the other end. This means you do not know whether the signal is being received at the other end, or whether the phone is off the hook.

As it buzzed successfully from the day it was installed, some two years ago, and now it does not buzz at the other end, I would like to know why, and why it cannot be restored to its original condition? The young man who was there today meant well, but I didn't quite understand his reasoning, therefore, can I ask you to restore the phones to as they originally were.

Likewise, up to today, when I left my home, when anybody buzzed me in my room, the phone did not buzz (this is in my room), however, I was told at my office today, over the telephone, it was buzzing when the Engineer tested it; this means it was faulty when I left my house, and suddenly it miraculously started to work again on its own. Can I, therefore, have a man to make sure that my phone buzzes, when it's buzzed from all the rooms in the house. This means that two men would have to come, one man to sit in one room, while the other man buzzes from all the other rooms to ascertain that it buzzes on the recipients phone, he then does it throughout the house, thus ensuring that no matter what phone is buzzed, it always buzzes at the receivers end.

If you like, I will stay at home on the day they are coming, and try and work with them to this end. I wonder if this can be done.

I must point out that these phones are very very temperamental, and I am wondering what their length of life is.

Anyhow, if you can ring me, either at the office and speak to ME, and if I am not there leave a message for me to phone you, if not can you phone me at home and speak to ME, if I'm not there, do leave a message that you have phoned.

Sincerely,

SPIKE MILLIGAN

19. If the said work shall become out of print and the Publishers shall fail to print and publish a new edition of at least 500 (five hundred) copies within 9 (nine) months of a written request from the Author to do so, then this Agreement shall automatically determine and the rights hereby granted shall revert to the Author subject only to the subsisting rights of any sub-licensee of the Publishers hereunder and to the continuing rights of the Publishers to their share of the proceeds from any sub-licences extant on the date of such reversion.

20. The Publishers agree to print the following words on the reverse of the title page:
.................(This indicates the actual year of original publication)
(c) ~~Spike Milligan~~ Productions 197

21. To keep the said work up-to-date the Author, if called upon by the Publishers, shall without charge to the Publishers edit and revise all editions of the said work during the currency of this Agreement and shall supply any new matter that may be necessary to that end. In the event of the Author neglecting or being unable by reason of death or otherwise to edit or revise the said work, or supply new matter where needed, the Publishers may engage some other person to edit or revise the said work or supply new matter, and may deduct the expense thereof from payments due to the Author under this Agreement.

22. If any difference shall arise between the Author and the Publishers touching the meaning of this Agreement or the rights and liabilities of the parties hereto the same shall be referred to the arbitration of two persons (one to be named by each party) or their mutually agreed umpire, in accordance with the provisions of the Arbitration Act 1950 or any statutory modification or re-enactment thereof for the time being in force.

23. It is hereby agreed that the Publisher shall have the first refusal (including the first opportunity to read and consider for publication) of the Author's next ....
works suitable for publication in volume form. Such work or works shall each be the subject of a fresh agreement between the Author and the Publisher, on terms which shall be fair and reasonable. If no terms shall have been agreed for its publication, the Author shall be at liberty to enter into an agreement with any other publisher provided that the Author shall not subsequently accept from anyone else less favourable terms than are offered by the Publisher.

The Publisher shall exercise this option within six weeks of receipt of the complete typescript or copy, except that he shall not be required to exercise it until two months after the publication of the work which is the subject of this Agreement.

Signed by

Signed by
*the.................
Author !

Director
MICHALL JOSLPH LTD

The 'above' the is a genuine
Spike Millgan 'the'.

Spike's idea of how to sign a book contract.

Spike and VAT

November 26.

Suffering VAT

From Mr Spike Milligan

Sir, Must we continue to suffer the energy-wasting, time-consuming lunacies of VAT, ie, I got a cheque from the BBC for £5—the cheque arrives in an envelope with a 6½p stamp? My manager then prepares a VAT invoice, this is sent back to the BBC on a 6½p stamp. The BBC then sends me a cheque for 40p with a 6½p stamp on, then we consider the original amount of £5 and the involvement of a BBC clerk, who sends it, the postman who delivers it, my manager who sends back the invoice, thus two postmen are involved, a secretary at the BBC to open it, without working out costs of the envelope, the paper and the printing, the time costs of the people involved, must surely come to *more* than the original amount of £5.

Of course, this doesn't take into account paying it into the bank, where the *cashier* is involved, and at the end of three months this one cheque is added to all others, then sent to the Customs and Excise. The ultimate was when a 40p VAT cheque arrived from the BBC unstamped—and 13p to pay.

I tell you the country is being run by LUNATICS!
Sincerely, one of the saner people,
SPIKE MILLIGAN.

November 29.

Spike wrote a letter to the newspapers, complaining about VAT. He received a reply from a Mr Vines saying it showed a lack of socialism. His answer:

9th December, 1976

To: Colin Vines Esq.

Dear Sir, (It was nice being called 'Dear Sir', normally in my Street I'm called 'Hey you').

Because I'm against V.A.T. apparently I am attacking socialism, so I suggest when the Conservatives come in, and I attack V.A.T. I will be attacking the Conservatives, and likewise when the Communists get in etc. etc.

You are obviously very deep into politics (I would say drowned), and when I say our leaders are lunatics, this is done in that healthy freedom of speech, which allows you to call a friend 'a silly old bugger'; that is democracy, and calling our leaders lunatics is done under the banner of democracy, which I can only hope the Socialists support.

If you have not got a sense of humour then all is lost, it's the 'heavies' in politics that treat everything as though it were a doctrine that cannot be deviated from.

Do you think I am the first person who ever called our leaders lunatics? It's repeated in pubs throughout the land ad nauseam every night.

I would have called anybody who introduced V.A.T. a lunatic, and may I point out to you V.A.T. was not introduced by a Labour Government, it was introduced by Mr Barber under a Conservative Government.

Again, can I clarify what I said, we are being run by lunatics, it was in reference to V.A.T. V.A.T. must have been the product of numerous Financial Committees who came to the conclusion that it was a good thing, so let us say you are right, and I am wrong.

If ever you watch one of my shows which is not funny, or read one of my books which is not funny, it is possibly due to the fact that much of my time is spent in filling in V.A.T. forms and filing, and in many cases, answering letters like yours.

I am going to conclude by saying that I was possibly a Socialist before you were; I was a member of the Young Socialists in 1933, and I was hit on the head by a rock in the Commercial Road, when we all joined forces to forestall Sir Edward Moseley and his Black shirts. I just mention this because some people think because you knock the people in power you are an anarchist.

Now, talking of lunacy, I really must quote what you have said in your letter, which actually admits we are being run by lunatics, and I quote: 'the Government has spent £2½ million on providing a new building in Plymouth for the employment of some more civil servants on a thing called a wealth tax – though unhappily the Government has not yet been able to *introduce* a wealth tax, and thus reduce the level of unemployment in Plymouth'. So, therefore, you admit the Government has spent £2½ million on a building which will be filled by civil servants, who have nothing to do. Really who's the lunatic – certainly not me.

I remain, dear Sir, yours sincerely,

SPIKE MILLIGAN

To: Sir Ronald Radford, KCB, MBE,
Customs & Excise   *10th December, 1976*

Dear Sir Ronald,

This letter is intended to try and save a lot of people a lot of time and a lot of paperwork.

My earnings as an entertainer/author etc. come in in various amounts during the course of the year. For each and every one of my appearances or writings I get a separate V.A.T. invoice. In the course of the year this can mean anything up to 2000 forms, even more. Would it not be intelligent to allow one Fiscal year, be it yours or mine to pass, and then add the grand total for one V.A.T. form which accommodates the whole lot?

Failing this, could it be done quarterly. Do let me know.

Sincerely,

SPIKE MILLIGAN

Sir Ronald Radford KCB MBE
Chairman

Board Room
H M Customs and Excise
King's Beam House
Mark Lane London EC3R 7HE

Our Ref: CPS 1748

S Milligan Esq
London W2

4 January 1977

Dear Mr Milligan.

You wrote to me on 10 December about the work involved in issuing
VAT invoices and suggesting that much work could be saved for all
concerned if, instead of issuing an invoice for each transaction,
you were permitted to prepare just one document at the end of each
year or, failing that, each quarter.

I appreciate that VAT does impose an additional burden on authors
and broadcasters, and I am concerned that this extra work should
be kept to a minimum. To this end, my department has already
agreed that an author or broadcaster working for the BBC may,
with the agreement of his local VAT office, issue his tax invoices
to them monthly. But we could not, I am afraid, adopt your
suggestion that only one document should be issued at the end
of each year or quarter. One important objection would be that
under such an arrangement each of your registered customers
would not hold the tax invoices he needs to produce to support
his claims to repayment of input tax.

I do assure you that we are constantly trying to simplify the
VAT procedures, and we are in fact currently discussing with
the BBC possible ways of further easing the VAT burden on their
contributors. In the meantime, if you wish to adopt the monthly
invoicing arrangements mentioned above, I would suggest that you
get in touch with your local VAT office at Wingate House,
93/107 Shaftesbury Avenue. I am sure they will do their best
to help you.

Yours sincerely,

RONALD RADFORD

*IF it
works
Monthly —
Why not
3
Monthly
I majored
in logic —
it was a
waste of
time*

Against Anthony Barbar
A resentment I harbour't
His introduction of VAT V-A-Tee
He has made life impossible for you & me
He himself has gone politically quiet
Is he on a vat-free diet?

Spike and the BBC

To: John Howard Davies Esq.,
Head of Comedy (Body & Legs to Follow),
British Broadcasting Corporation

2nd September, 1982

Dear John,

Thank you for your condolences, but it was too late, last night I killed myself.

Goodbye,

SPIKE MILLIGAN

P.S. A wreath would be a comfort, provided it is signed by the entire staff of BBC 2.

Spike serenading Michael Parkinson

To: Michael Parkinson Esq.,
British Broadcasting Corporation   *11th November, 1981*

Dear Michael,

   I hear I am to be on your show again, I think this time I must get a marble clock, and a citation for a lifetime of service to Michael Parkinson, and overseas service in Australia.

   I look forward to this occasion as my dear friend Michael Foot is on the programme.

   I will turn up in a raiment of rags to try and make him look well dressed.

                                   Love, light and peace,

                                   SPIKE MILLIGAN

To: John Howard Davies Esq.   *18th November, 1982*

Dear John,

Your annual appeal to try and get people to come to your Christmas Party has arrived. I notice this year there has been no payment included in the invitation to attract us.

One question – this year do we bring sandwiches and a thermos of tea as we usually do. I mean, I only want to help the show be a success, and I will bring a sprig of Holly which you will find very handy for putting on the chairs of anybody you don't like.

Love, light and peace,

SPIKE MILLIGAN

P.S. I hope you are not inviting that terrible Lord Howard, I suppose it's better than having Billy Connolly there, still I will try and be nice to him and I will be bringing a spare wheel for his wheelchair.

Opposite: He's upset the stage door manager again (1980)

To: Ian Anthony Esq.,
British Broadcasting Corporation   *1st April, 1982*

Dear Ian,

Thank you for making a glorious cock-up of the timings between Australia and England, which resulted in phoning my brother whilst he was asleep, and possibly the worst fucking interview I have ever had in my life.

We must do it again sometime.

Sincerely,

SPIKE MILLIGAN

Ian Anthony replied: 'I don't know which of the bastards I work with gave you my name, but I had nothing to do with arranging your interview', and he suggested they had dinner.

To: Ian Anthony Esq.   *20th April, 1982*

Dear Ian,

Mea Culpa. So, the cock up about the cock ups are still going on.

Yes, I would love you to take me to dinner, and you can tell me (a) who you are (b) how dare you have a sense of humour and work for a crowd of creeps like the B.B.C., and (c) I can tell you why I have a sense of humour and work for a crowd of creeps like the B.B.C., and (d) I can possibly glean some stories for my final book 'Aunty' which is now reaching massive proportions and should demolish the whole of the B.B.C. on the first day of publication.

Love, light and peace,

SPIKE MILLIGAN

Spike and the
House of Commons

To Dr David Owen, MP   *14th April, 1981*

Dear David Owen,

I much appreciate the stand you have taken on tobacco and alcohol. Essentially smokers are nicotine junkies and are every bit drug addicts as say, cocaine sniffers are, so consequently the placing of the words 'cigarettes can seriously damage your health' on the side of packets of cigarettes is as ineffectual as calling reveille in a graveyard.

The essential thing is to stop the habit at source. We all know that 90% of this takes place in school. It takes very little money to introduce a programme into schools whereby children already addicted (and some are by the age of 13) should be warned, and this is the important part, that if they are caught passing on the habit they will be expelled. Likewise the parents should be informed of this discipline. This is stern stuff, but we are dealing with a practice which could introduce lung cancer to another human being. In an indirect way these people are performing sociological murders.

Love, light and peace,

SPIKE MILLIGAN

From: The Rt.Hon. Dr. David Owen MP

HOUSE OF COMMONS
LONDON SWIA OAA

16th April 1981

Spike Milligan, Esq.,

London W2

Dear Spike Milligan,

Thank you for your letter. I enclose for your interest a copy of what
I actually said.

I would welcome headmasters and headmistresses of schools taking a
tougher attitude on smoking, but whether they should expel people is
for them to decide and seems to be to be pretty extreme, with a
lot of social consequences since another school would have to take them.

What I think is a better approach is the factual explanation, preferably
by a doctor, with those horrible pathological pots of cancerous growth.
If a school teacher tells a youngster not to smoke there tends to be a
reaction against authority and to do the opposite. Family doctors could
do a lot more in my view in terms of health education as well as sex
education.

With best wishes,

Yours sincerely,

David Owen

[handwritten annotations:]

No one **Lures** them to stop
so –? They smoke –
what's the difference in
telling them –

Dear David – Pretty Extreme.
Yes – pretty extreme David –
I **wny canull** is Pretty extreme
No one is **We** actually
know in

To: Dr David Owen, MP   22nd April, 1981

Dear David Owen,

Thank you for your letter; I will have one more try.

'Expelling pupils seems to be pretty extreme.' Well of course it is my dear David, passing on lung cancer is a pretty extreme thing to do. They would be forewarned on a very amicable basis, of the procedure which would be taken in the event of making non-smoking pupils take up the habit. We are not penalising the smokers we are trying to kill that pernicious school boy trick of daring the innocent to take it up.

I have had dozens of letters like yours showing disagreement with the idea, and therefore, I feel rather like a voice crying in the wilderness, and in 30 years time when the habit is still persisting, I do hope you will think I had a point at this early stage.

Conclusion speech: no one, anywhere, is actually tackling the problem at source.

Thanks for writing anyhow.

Sincerely,

SPIKE MILLIGAN

From: The Rt Hon Dr David Owen MP

HOUSE OF COMMONS
LONDON SW1A OAA

5 May 1981

Spike Milligan Esq

London W2

Dear Spike Milligan

Many thanks for your further letter. The
problem is that the very pupils most likely
to risk all and smoke and the very ones
who would most like to be expelled. Then
having expelled them what do you do?

Yours sincerely

David Owen

To: The Rt Hon Dr David Owen   *8th May, 1981*

Dear David,

O.K. David, the continuing story of Owen versus Milligan. Re the pupils who obviously delight in being expelled. Bearing in mind, prior to this, the parents and the pupils are all warned of the consequences of passing on the smoking habit, and therefore, it's their choice, with their parents knowledge as to what the outcome will be, and what is more important David, we have got rid of the barbarians who are giving lung cancer to other children. Desperate circumstances demand desperate measures, hence the desperate result of my proposals. Mind you, they might not wish to be expelled. I don't think there is going to be a mass exodus and expellings because all smokers are not psychologically geared towards leaving school.

We won't pursue this further, but in ten years time, my dear David, when the problem is still there, do bear in mind what I have said.

Fresh approach – I am at a political dalliance as to who to vote for at the next election, if your Party has in its Manifesto a positive scheme towards population stabilisation and even reduction (horror, horror, hands in the air), I might be interested to support you, and I might say I have a large abstract following of people who would be influenced if I choose to support the Social Democratic Party. Do let me know.

At the moment, for God's sake don't tell Michael Foot.

Love, light and peace,

SPIKE MILLIGAN

Seal rally in Trafalgar Square

To: The Rt Hon. Mrs Margaret Thatcher, PM
10 Downing Street,
LONDON SW1   7th December, 1982

Dear Mrs Thatcher,

I had a sighting of your reply to the R.S.P.C.A.'s letter of the 18th October, 1982 regarding the seal ban. You quote that you and your Government would only consider a ban on seal products if it shows that the species is proven to be endangered.

I hate to draw this parallel but whereas the human race is not an endangered species, you showed a remarkable amount of compassion, and even shed tears of concern at the thought of even the loss of one of them, namely your son, Mark Thatcher. Dare I say, what would you have done if you had to wait for a Scientific Committee to sit in judgement for a decision on whether he was worth saving. Basically the argument is a moral one. Man is the only creature who has a chance to show compassion through his morality.

I speak prophetically, the human race can no longer continue the course of believing that animals have to give way to them. When you consider the sheer slaughter and massacre of the Jews by the Germans, and even nearer to date, the slaughter of innocent Palestinians, by what are laughingly called 'Christian' Phalangists in the Lebanon.

I beg you to have some compassion in your judgement, and not rely solely on committees. Don't be like Pontius Pilate and wash your hands of the matter.

Meanwhile, I take this opportunity of wishing you and your family a very Merry Christmas.

Love, light and peace,

SPIKE MILLIGAN

To: The Rt Hon. Norman St John Stevas, MP

8th March, 1983

Dear Norman,

A few months ago, I was standing outside No. 10, with an appeal against the killing of baby seals in Canada, and I remember you passing me and laughingly saying 'if it's one of your causes, it must be a lost one'.

I think you will see, if you read your newspapers, that the EEC, as a result of pressure 'with our lost causes', have brought about a volte face, in that they are going to ban the slaughter of baby seals. I just thought I would commit coup on you, Norman.

Watch out for further forthcoming lost causes, i.e. the flooding of the Franklin River, etc.

You realise, of course, I am only writing to you because like myself you are a Catholic. Poor Malcolm Muggeridge was driven from the Protestant faith by the organ playing of Richard Ingrams.

Love, light and peace,

SPIKE MILLIGAN

HOUSE OF COMMONS
LONDON SWIA OAA

24th March 1983

My dear Spike,

    Thank you so much for your note -
in this cause I support you 100%.
Well done.

            All blessings,

            + Nu.SfJl.

Spike Milligan, Esq

To: Lord Carrington, KC, MG, MC,
Secretary of State for the Foreign
& Commonwealth Office   *30th March, 1982*

Dear Lord Carrington,

   Just to congratulate you and your Foreign Office on it's 200th Anniversary.

Thought you would like one from a clown.

                              Love, light and peace,

                              SPIKE MILLIGAN

To: The Rt Hon. Mrs Margaret Thatcher, PM,
10 Downing Street,
LONDON, SW1   *22nd January, 1982*

Dear Mrs Thatcher,

Me again. Reading between the lines, I think the resignation of Mr Nicholas Fairbairn is really due to pressure coming from you, and I think if this is so, I must congratulate you on the Government acting so quickly on something which is causing inflammatory feeling among the public.

It was indeed a wise move, and I trust his replacement will have more perspicacity on this subject.

I told you Mark would come back, didn't I, apparently he forgot to take a razor.

Sincerely,

SPIKE MILLIGAN

177

```
                                          SOCIALIST COUNTRYSIDE GROUP.
THE RT HON: MICHAEL FOOT.                                      26.3.83
CONWAY HALL. RED LION SQUARE.  LONDON

CAN'T BE WITH YOU ON THIS IMPORTANT OCCASION.  THE REST OF
THE WQRLD MAY THINK LITTLE OF THIS OCCASION BUT IF I
REMEMBER THAT'S EXACTLY WHAT LINCOLN THOUGHT ABOUT THE
GETTISBERG ADDRESS.  LET'S HOPE THE SAME APPLIES TO THIS
OCCASION.  THE LAND AND ANIMALS OF THIS WORLD ARE CRYING
OUT FOR HELP.  LET US TRY AND GIVE IT TO THEM.  REMEMBER
THE LESS PEOPLE THE BIGGER THE WORLD WILL BECOME.


LOVE SPIKE MILLIGAN
```

Spike and Children

KING
BLACKBOTTOM

Spike received a letter from Mrs M.H. Reith, Northview Junior Mixed School saying that they had been examining their library books for any that contained anything racially or sexually offensive. Spike's children's book, *Dip the Puppy*, contained a character called King Blackbottom, so she informed him they were recommending to the Director of Education that *Dip the Puppy* be excluded from all school and children's libraries in the Borough of Brent.
Spike's reply:

To: Mrs M.H. Reith,
London Borough of Brent Education Committee,
Northview Junior Mixed & Infants School   *3rd June, 1982*

Dear Mrs Reith,

If you feel free to remove the book because of the mention of 'KING BLACKBOTTOM', I am a complete believer in freedom; but you don't sound as though you are enjoying it.

Love, light and peace,

SPIKE MILLIGAN

P.S. Perhaps if I had put 'KING WHITEBOTTOM'.

To: The Children of Class 7J,
Manor Field Junior School   *26th January, 1978*

Dear Children of Class 7J,

What a lovely surprise to get all your letters and drawings. I went through all of them, and they were all lovely drawings.

I think your teacher is very lucky to have such a lot of talented children in her classroom, and I think one of you will grow up to be the Prime Minister, and give all the children seven days holiday from school a week, and for those who can't add, eight days holiday a week.

Here's a poem for you:

> There was a young girl called Nellie
> Who had a nylon belly
> The skin was so thin,
> We could all see in,
> And inside was custard and jelly,

Love, from

UNCLE SPIKE

Opposite: Entertaining the troops in my office (1979)

182

TO SPIKE WITH LOVE

Maureen and Bill Smith of Motueka were off to London today with the hope of giving this signed book to British comedian and writer Spike Milligan.

It has been signed by all the cast of "Badjelly the Witch", including the 35 child actors and singers aged from 6-15. Maureen and Bill want to tell Spike about the importance of entertainment for children in Motueka and how important a play like "Badjelly" is.

More than 1500 people packed the four shows of "Badjelly" at the weekend. At the Sunday matinee, more than 70 people had to be turned away, including some crying children.

Mr and Mrs Smith said later they were distressed that people had to be turned away but there was simply no room in the Memorial Hall for them.

Because of other commitments among the cast, it was impossible to organise an extra performance.

All 350 seats in the Memorial Hall were filled for the other performances and forms had to be brought in for extra people. One father arrived from Golden Bay on Saturday afternoon with seven children and no tickets. They had made the crossing over the Takaka Hill through snow in the hope of getting into the show.

The Smiths are taking Spike a book of coloured photos of New Zealand donated by the Grand Book Store, photos of the show and a clipping of the review.

The Smiths, Merseysiders from Birkenhead, are making their first trip to Britain after 18 years here. As well as meeting Spike Milligan they hope to find out about other possible children's productions.

They also hope to see the West End shows "Evita" and "Cats".

184

To: Motueka Production of Badjelly,
New Zealand   *18th August, 1982*

Dear Badjelliers,

I am stunned at the success of Badjelly the Witch in the distant Colonies. Last time I was there they had ony just stopped eating Missionaries, and that was in 1979.

Thank you all for that wonderful book.

Remember, over population is what will kill your Country like it did India, so keep your numbers down and your chins up.

Love, light and peace,

SPIKE MILLIGAN

Spike and the Rest of the World

Spike wrote a letter to *Private Eye* objecting to the mosque in Regents Park. He received a reply from Helen Slyomovics and Barry Wilkins saying he was a racist. His answer to their accusation:

To: Helen Slyomovics & Barry Wilkins   *23rd August, 1977*

Dear Helen and Barry,

I am not a racist, the word is used too easily these days, one can blaspheme at the English (Pommie Bastard), at the Irish (Irish jokes about them being stupid), etc. etc. – no one says racist, but it becomes almost an automatic reaction to shout racist to anybody who says anything about Pakistanis, or negroes, etc.

Well, absorb very carefully what I am about to write, and you may understand my letter in Private Eye.

So, I object to a Mosque in Regents Park, to you this means I am a Racist, O.K. I also object to Gothic Churches that have been built in India, does this mean I am a racist as well, if so, then I also hate the English. If you say 'yes', to the last mentioned, don't read any further.

Because, like many people you have become over sensitised, like the people who say, that even if proven and a black murderer is judged guilty, and the jury happens to be white, there are those creeps who shout the jury are racist.

One cannot arrest coloured people anymore, even justifiably without creeps shouting out 'he's a racist'. I am all for each race surviving, I volunteered to fight in the Six Day Israeli War, not to be overwhelmed by the Arabs. Likewise, I also stood for a homeland for the Palestinian people, but what I object to is the destruction of the environment by architecture, which has no harmony with the surroundings. I think a Mosque in the middle of London looks bloody awful, and if you don't think so, then you have no eye for beauty, and we have absolutely nothing in common. Obviously you would like a Zulu Resting Camp in Hyde Park, so I hope one day they will build one there, so it will please you.

Sincerely, *SPIKE MILLIGAN*

Who once stood on the lines at Whitechapel against Oswald Moseley in 1933.

To: *Sir George Jefferson, CBE,*
Chairman,
British Telecom   *5th November, 1981*

Dear Sir George,

   The attached letter is self-explanatory. While we have communications a plenty orbiting around the world in space, I can't dial out, even to Finchley, on my own phone on earth.

   Don't send an Engineer round to see my phone they have done that several times. The phone is O.K., it's somewhere in the exchange where the fault is.

   I write to you because I have tried every other means, except Prince Philip, he's next.

                                        Sincerely,

                          SPIKE MILLIGAN

To: *The Accounts Manager,*
London North Telephone Area   *5th November, 1981*

Dear Sir,

                  re: *TELEPHONE NO.* ——

   I am not paying my bill whenever it comes up, because for nearly three months I have had a fault on my telephone. I have reported it frequently and until it is rectified to my satisfaction, I can't pay the bill because I have to go through the operators, who I think are charging me for each call.

                                        Sincerely,

                          SPIKE MILLIGAN

British
TELECOM

from the Chairman
Sir George Jefferson CBE

British Telecommunications

2-12 Gresham Street
LONDON
EC2V 7AG

Telephone
National _____
International   + 44

Telex 883051

Prestel Page 383

SPIKE TOOK LETTER
5/11/81
GOT BACK.

10 December 1981

Dear Mr Milligan,

Thank you for your letter of 5 November and the copy of your letter
to the Accounts Manager of our London North Area which was enclosed.

I was sorry to learn of the difficulties which you have been
experiencing recently with your telephone service. The equipment
at the local telephone exchange, associated with your line, has
been tested thoroughly and no faults have been found which would
have given rise to the trouble which you have experienced.

I understand that your service is now satisfactory. However, the
local Service Manager, Mr O'Connor on 01-340 8060 Ext 7260, will be
keeping your service under review and he will be pleased to help
should the need arise in the future.

In view of the additional use which you have had to make of the
operator service, arrangements are being made to reduce your next
bill accordingly.

I should be grateful if you would accept my apologies for the
inconvenience which these difficulties have caused.

Yours sincerely,

SIR GEORGE JEFFERSON

WHS Distributors

A division of W.H.Smith & Son Limited

Sales office and services
St. John's House
East Street
Leicester LE1 6NE

Telephone: (0533) 551196
Telex: 341415 WHSDSJ G

Distribution offices and warehouse
Euston Street
Freemen's Common
Aylestone Road
Leicester LE2 7SS

Telephone: (0533) 547671/5
Telex: 341960 WHSDIS G

From: S R Morgan
Assistant Sales Manager - Stationery Division

18 November 1982
SRM/CV

Dear Spike

Jill Tomalin, the pen buyer for W H Smith, mentioned to me
this week that you had purchased, and were pleased with the
Sanford Calligraphic pen that we distribute in the UK.

To show our delight that such an eminent philosopher, historian,
wit and raconteur should be satisfied with our product please
accept with my compliments the enclosed gift sets, and a few
of our new fine point calligraphic pens.

With all good wishes to you and the exploding nuns,

Yours sincerely

Steve Morgan

22nd November, 1982

Dear Steve,

The very name strikes terror in the human heart – you are, of course, a direct descendant of the Pirate Captain Morgan, who was found to possess a case of stolen pens from some poor American Tea Clipper on its way to a simple Atomic Testing Range.

But seriously, it was a splendid gesture on your part (I have some very splendid gestures on my parts, all done by a local Tattooist).

Yes, the pens are marvellous and it will help improve the calligraphy of a nation whose handwriting I find appalling. On the subject of calligraphy, I have a Doctor who writes in the most beautiful copper-plate hand, and I said to him 'what splendid writing', and he hung his head, and said 'yes, I am a disgrace to my profession'.

Again Steve, thank you for the gesture.

I presume by your name you might be Welsh, only I am a Rugger Maniac.

Love, light and peace,

SPIKE MILLIGAN

Spike received a circular letter from London Borough of Barnet asking him to cut his hedge as it was 'overhanging the footpath'.
His reply:

To: A.J. Stringer Esq.,
London Borough of Barnet   *18th November, 1982*

Dear Mr Stringer,

You poor devil having to write letters about over-hanging hedges.

You see, what I am trying to do is to block the path of those Pakistanis, that pass through in caravans behind my house with their camels, goats and tents. Of course, I will try to cut it now, you having discovered my secret trap, I will have it done by a man with manicure scissors to help the current unemployment so popular in Finchley.

I hope all goes well with all the poor lads in the Council. I noticed the Town Clerk last Saturday in the shopping centre with a begging bowl, trying to raise funds for a new suit. We will have to get rid of Margaret Thatcher.

Best regards for the season.

Sincerely,

SPIKE MILLIGAN

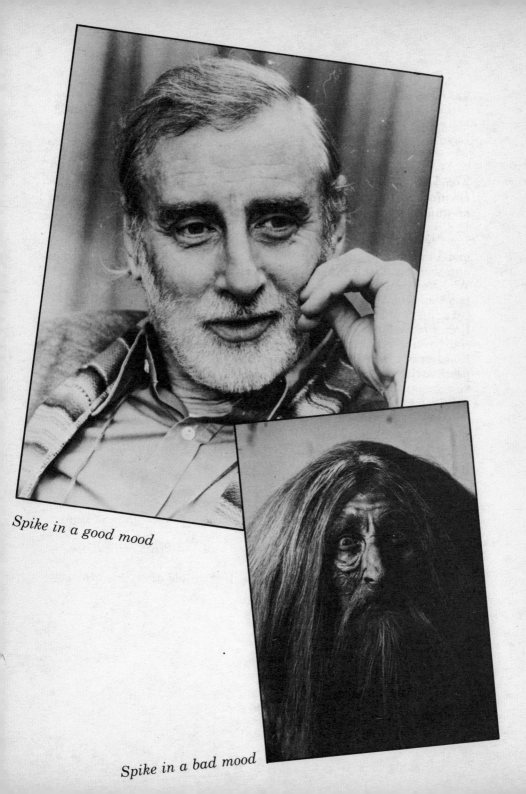

Spike in a good mood

Spike in a bad mood

Dear Sir,

I received a most disorganised phone call from somebody at St. Andrews University, who waited until I had gone to Ireland to phone me, from a coin box, and through the insertions of the 10p. I gathered he wanted me to be Rector of St. Andrews.

I tentatively said 'yes', as he appeared to be running out of 10p., and I asked him to send full details to my office. Can I ask some questions about this lunatic: Why does he wait until I come to Ireland? Why does he wait until I come off the stage, dripping with sweat from a two hour One Man Show. It was like going into a boxing ring, when the boxer has just been knocked out, and asking him 'Would you like to be Rector of St. Andrews University'. All this, plus the fact he was in a coin box, inserting 10p made it very difficult to know if such a degree of chaos really warranted a Rector, I would gladly become resident psychiatrist at St. Andrews if it would help.

Do let me know more about it, and try not to phone me when I am on tour, I will be back in London at the end of November.

All in all he could not have picked a worse time to get an answer.

Can you please write lucidly, and tell me what it is all about, and exactly what it entails.

Love, light and peace,

SPIKE MILLIGAN

P.S. I know that St. Andrew was crucified upside down, has this got something to do with it.

He received a reply from Andrew Bell giving more details:

To: Andrew D. Bell Esq.,
SRC Office,
Students Union,
St. Andrews   *22nd October, 1982*

Dear Andrew,

When you spoke to me on the telephone I was at a disadvantage, in as much I was not prepared for this offer. Nor could I get all it entailed from your brief conversation. Your letter points out more detail, and I find that the Rectorship is too strenuous for me to accept, in as much as I don't have as much spare time as Tim Brooke-Taylor and Frank Muir. This does not mean I don't want to accept it, I would have been delighted to accept it.

Alas, I am a seven day a week man, up to my neck in work and family – let this coming as a warning to all of you!! It's time that scoundrels were given the Rectorship, what about John De Lorean, he needs cheering up at the moment, to the tune of 50 million pounds, and think of the cheap hash that could come the way of your dear students.

Again Andrew, thank you for offering, I am desperately sorry to have to say no.

Sincerely,

SPIKE MILLIGAN

197

Father Patrick Fury told Spike in 1975 that their friendship must end. This is Spike's attempt to re-establish communication. It did:

Dear Pat,

Perhaps by now you 'Fury' at me over the Pope will have cooled, people are allowed opinions, and I was voicing mine, if I were to be angered by every opinion I didn't agree with I would die of apoplexy. In case you were not aware, I still consider myself a 'thinking' Christian, and I therefore disagree with much of the Papal Dogma, because it starts to become ridiculous in the

light of a changing world, and I don't
want it to be ridiculous, so I have to speak
up, after all Jesus did, he spoke out against
his own religion – I'm sure many faithful
religious Jews must have reacted very much
the way you reacted to me. I still haven't
changed, but I dislike being at odds with
you because you are a nice man –
If I'm in Liverpool again – would you have
dinner with me
                    Love, Light & Peace
                    Spike Milligan

To: *The Rt Hon. Malcolm Fraser, CH, MP,*
Prime Minister,
Australia   *14th January, 1983*

Dear Mr Fraser,

Your intervention in the holding process against the Franklin River Dam Scheme is indeed a most enlightened one.

I have been keeping a close watch on the statistics in the struggle and basically, believe me, the majority of Tasmanians do not want it.

I plead with you to please continue your holding process and ignore, what I consider, some environmental ignoramuses. There's an old saying among Western people, when local Government Councils meet and don't know what to do on that day, someone always says:– 'Eh, why don't we build a Dam.'

Again, I cannot commend you highly enough for your attitude. Tasmania is, as you know, among one of the last great wildernesses; kept so it could bring in great revenues from tourists in years to come.

I am sorry that no rain is falling on your farm, it might be something to do with the number of trees that have been logged in Australia since the beginning of Colonisation.

I hope all goes well with you for the New Year, and I wish you:

Love, light and peace to you and your family,

SPIKE MILLIGAN

P.S. Congratulations on the Ashes.

To: Tony Banks Esq.,
Chairman, Arts & Recreation Committee,
Greater London Council

8th March, 1983
(Dictd. 4/3/83).

Dear Tony,

I am about to depart for Australia and New Zealand, I presume by the time I get there Bob Hawke, the Labour Leader will almost certainly have won the election.

This is just my last attempt to, on my parting, remind you of Coombe Cliff. I have seen the model prepared for what it would look like insitu in Horniman Gardens. If it comes off I would be willing to get very good coverage for the G.L.C. (that's if it is still Labour).

Alas, I might as well tell you I have had an altercation with Ken Livingstone's secretary, Karen, who always acts in the most off-hand way with me, she pontificates when Ken Livingstone is not there as though she was his Chief Deputy, all of which is a pain in the arse when you are trying to help.

Only the other day I gave Ken Livingstone very good coverage on Morning Television when the Press were giving him a hammering. In the wake of that I was phoning to ask him not to forget Coombe Cliff, but his secretary, Karen seemed as useful as Hitler in a Synagogue.

Anyhow, I have spoken to your secretary, who also seems as interested in me as taking strychnine, so I have left a message for you to phone me, but, of course, she thinks you are busy, if she knew what my life was like, she would think you were on holiday all the time.

Anyway, it is an attempt to do something for England, not bad from an Irishman.

Love, light and peace,

SPIKE MILLIGAN

P.S. Get a new secretary.

Rehearsing to become Lord Mayor of London

To: Ken Livingstone Esq.,
Greater London Council

8th March, 1983
(Dictd. 4/3/83).

Dear Ken,

I am writing to say I have given up trying to contact you, because whenever I phone it is always with something important, in this case Coombe Cliff, and I consistently get the feeling from your secretary, Karen, who seems to officiate as if she was your representative, and always gives me the feeling of total indifference to the interest I am showing in something. I am doing this voluntarily.

Originally she said, with reference to the first meeting I had – Ah this has been passed over to Tony Banks – and when I phoned Tony Banks he knew nothing about it. Madam was continuing on the phone as the Leader of the G.L.C., and I resented her pontificating attitude. Believe me I can make much more money than talking to secretaries, and it doesn't do the G.L.C. any good.

On this occasion I phoned to ask if I could speak to you about Coombe Cliff, immediately the barrier came up 'it's nothing to do with' etc. etc., and I wasn't asking her what to do, what I was wanting was to pass a message on to you, at which stage I really lost my temper, because on that morning, I had taken special care to give you a very good coverage on Breakfast Television, which you were not getting in the Press and when I came up against an attitude like Karen's, I feel, in future, I will vote SDP.

I won't bother you, or shall I say, I won't bother her anymore. She's just lost a very good friend to the G.L.C.

Likewise, I have tried Tony Banks, who has a secretary of the same ilk. No wonder the Conservative Government want to abolish you.

If you are going to win the battle, at least brief your staff to appear to be interested when somebody is doing something for and on behalf of their Country, i.e. England.

Sincerely,

SPIKE MILLIGAN

Dear Egon,

I went to the Café Royal last week, and I would like to make a few comments. I ate in the Le Relais Restaurant. I had been to the Opera, and I was in evening dress, and to see a Sommelier literally sloshing wine into the glass, and almost filling it to the brim, with complete indifference for his job, is something I should report.

I ordered Scampi Provençal, and I should imagine the process of it coming, went something like this. You get an army boot, and put a carpet of scampi inside. You send it with a soldier to the Falkland Islands for the Battle of Goose Green. When he has done his duty, he will then post it back to you, and the scampi will then be dropped into a kettle of boiling water for several days, scooped out, then served steaming hot with a tomato sauce to a victim called Spike Milligan. The effect of the scampi on the palate was as if it had been fired from a cannon, repeatedly against the walls of Pevensey Castle. As Oscar Wilde would have put it, they were fucking awful.

Sincerely,

SPIKE MILLIGAN

SOLIDARITY WITH SOLIDARITY   13TH MARCH 1983

I CAN'T BE WITH YOU TODAY. I WANT TO SAY A NATION
CANNOT BE HELD IN THRALL. ONE DAY THE DOMINATION
WILL END BUT UNTIL THAT END THE STRUGGLE FOR THE
FREEDOM OF THE POLISH PEOPLE MUST GO ON.

POLAND IS FULL OF SUFFERING AND EVERYBODY IN THE
FREE WORLD MUST TAKE A SHARE OF IT.

BEST WISHES TO THIS OCCASION LET FREEDOM THROUGH
SOLIDARITY WIN.

LOVE, LIGHT AND PEACE, SPIKE MILLIGAN

To: Sir George Jefferson, CBE,
British Telecommunications   1st June, 1982

Dear Sir,

I write to you, and perhaps you could possibly pass this down the line to the requisite department.

On Saturday, 29th May, at 7-00 a.m. a lorry drove up outside my home, and for the next one and a half hours made the most deafening noise while hauling underground cables through the sewers.

I know people have to work, but to pick the one day of rest, that me and my family have, and most people are asleep at that time, I find it appallingly insensitive, and I am certain a small change in the time schedules could be made so that a more sociable hour could be chosen.

It's very simple, if they do it again I will set fire to the lorry – I'm not joking.

Sincerely,

SPIKE MILLIGAN

British
TELECOM

From the Chairman
Sir George Jefferson CBE

British Telecommunications

2-12 Gresham Street
LONDON
EC2V 7AG

Telephone
National   01- 357 3000
International
                +44 I 357 3000
Telex 883051

Prestel Page 383

Dear Spike /

Sorry about the noise on 29 May.

It won't happen again.

But just in case, I enclose a box of matches, with
British Telecom's compliments.

Yours sincerely

George

To: Harrow Road Police Station   *1st September, 1978*

Dear Lads,

The petrol cap was knocked off during the carnival. I hear some of the lads had their caps knocked off as well. Drop in any time for tea, you are always welcome. Despite the knockers you are the best.

As ever

SPIKE

To: Peter Cookson Esq.   *4th March, 1982*

Dear Master Carpenter,

I have received your bill for two million pounds for putting the shelf in the carsey. I did find this a bit steep, not the bill, but the angle of the shelf. So, I will be going to the International Lending Fund to raise the two million to pay for this job.

In the meantime, I'm sending you £80, not £70, as you asked, but £10 will cover inflation while the money is in transit.

I will be considering your charges for leaping on and off walls, drinking tea, and being attacked by the house cat.

You will be hearing from my Solicitor in the morning, which is more than I bloody well do.

I am keeping your letter because it's so funny.

As ever,

SPIKE MILLIGAN

The reason the master carpenter's letter is not here – Spike really did keep it.

DEPARTMENT OF HEALTH AND SOCIAL SECURITY

DHSS

Reference _ST/MI_

3.2.1982

Mr. T. A. MILLIGAN

PADDINGTON
LONDON W2.

Dear Sir or Madam

We need to up-date out reards Therefore

~~To help us to deal as quickly as possible with your claim for benefit.~~

would you please let me have* _your._
birth certificate. Please send or bring it _with this letter;_ the certificate
will be returned to you as soon as we have finished with it.

If you do not have the certificate please give the particulars asked for
on the back of this letter and return it to me so that I can, if appropriate,
ask for a search to be made in the records of the Registrar General.

An addressed ~~label~~ _envelope_ is enclosed.

Yours faithfully

Manager

Form MF 2
(Env EW 18)

*Indicate whose certificate

Your ref. ST/MI.
To: The Manager,
Department of Health & Social Security　　　*16th February, 1982*

Dear Sir,

Thank you for your letter of the 3rd February. I don't understand why you need my birth certificate to up-date your records. My original birth date, which you accepted, still stands, you can't up-date a birth, one only has one birthday.

Sincerely,

SPIKE MILLIGAN

To: Department of Health & Social Security,
Child Benefit Centre   *19th January, 1983*

Dear Sirs,

Help, shock, horror. Last year you asked if my daughter Jane, aged 16 years, was to continue with her education. At that time she had decided she wanted to continue her 'O' Levels at Barnet College, and I have been receiving child allowance, she has now decided to work and not attend the college, so I am in receipt of the allowance criminally. I do not wish to spend a year in Broadmoor because of this, so will you please cancel the payments, and I'm enclosing herewith my Order Book.

You lucky devils, I might have to send you back some money, and that ought to cheer the country up no end.

My daughter started work on the 1st November, 1982.

I hope you are going to be nice about this, otherwise I will have another six children, and that will put some paperwork in your way, you see I still have the equipment.

Sincerely,

SPIKE MILLIGAN

Form CH 103

Department of Health and Social Security

Child Benefit Centre (Washington)

PO Box 1   Newcastle upon Tyne   NE88 1AA

27/CM

Mr T A Milligan

Bayswater
LONDON W2

Your reference

Our reference
CHB 74745826 LG

Date
31ˢᵗ January 1983

Dear Mr Milligan

Thank you for your letter dated 19 January 1983. I must
say that I appreciate your sense of humour.

As a result of your daughter's change in circumstances
you have been overpaid child benefit amounting to £57.30.
Will you therefore let me have your cheque for that amount.

Yours sincerely

F E JACKSON

To: F.E. Jackson Esq.,
Department of Health & Social Security,
Child Benefit Centre   *2nd February, 1983*

Dear Mr Jackson,

Thank you for your letter of the 31st January. Please find enclosed herewith cheque for £57.29, would you like to sue me for the remainder, so by the time you have a heart attack, at the discrepancy of 1p., I have tried to remedy it by sending you a free copy of one of my books.

Love, light and peace,

SPIKE MILLIGAN

P.S. Supposing my daughter wants to go back to school – what then? Does this mean you send me back the £57.29, if you do, I will sue you because I know for a fact that the amount is a penny short.

6/BD

Form CH 103B

Department of Health and Social Security
Child Benefit Centre (Washington)
PO Box 1 Newcastle upon Tyne NE88 1AA

Mr T A Milligan

Bayswater
LONDON W2

Your reference

Our reference
CHB 74745826 LG

Date

4 February 1983

Dear Mr Milligan

Thank you for your letter and cheque of 2 February 1983 and for the gift which is much appreciated. The effect of receiving your book has left me tittering with excitement but unfortunately I am not in a position to return the compliment - not many people would like a copy of the Child Benefit Act and Regulations especially a copy autographed by F E Jackson - who is he?

Initially the receipt of your package caused quite a stir after being mistaken for a letter bomb but with the experts on the job it was soon "defused". You could say that the launching of your book in the Child Benefit Centre went off with a bang.

Anyway, when the word was out fellow workers came from all directions just to gaze at your work of art, so you see folks shrewdness has paid off again and no doubt the sale of your book will increase in this part of the country. You lucky fellow. Any discount for civil servants?

Joking aside, if you have any further problems regarding any child benefit matter please do not hesitate to let me know and once again, thanks.

Yours sincerely

FRANK E JACKSON

SPINE

A HUMAN BEING.

hoever.